Statistically speaking, they're all the same person.

(But we're not about statistics.)

Hap... ...eview!

we ... ...53, ...by one
... ...uac.

...er
...Can:
... Jack
... White

By now, at ...
reluctant to le...
dawn: the giga...
rise, and becom...
Read this d...
ters on Saturda...
circled in dark...
to the human vo...
to the unravel...
at the hands of...
rings of darkne...
fondly in fond...
of safe, soft c...
sat, and at the...
places whe... W...
mice hide,
dwelling o...
is a man.)

"They sat ...
at mid-point b...
then leaned fo...
bit their fing...
laboured to he...
laughed, roare...
thing. Even t...
revery, and hi...
derstanding.

"It was a ...
by radios all ...
and is sewing ...
mixing drinks ...
at the Rainbow...
on the parlor ...
with wagons glow...
same warm glow...
shots and s... T...
all around
nigs-and-ma...
places where ...
child-sweet.

"Yet t... C...
some kind—...
tive himself,
who snarled in...
he listened t...
he knew that ...
everywhere: w...
gloated for je...

"Yup. ...
in the rockin...
---But...
"For k...
city like St.
out front wit...
ideas!---"
These l...
a true, thoug...
Come on, Ed W...
madness. But...
Who gives a fuck anyway. Write a madder letter if
you can.   So long boy, *Jack*

...etters
...published
...or, wit,
...oughts,
...ver the
...ars. Written
...over their
...bia through
...Kerouac's

It was a visit with White in Denver
that began the *On the Road* journeys, and it was White who suggested the literary
sketching technique that helped Kerouac achieve the fast, intuitive prose style for
which he became known. Vivid samples of this characteristic approach are present
in these letters, passages of which made their way into his novels. They are the
rough drafts that Kerouac said he didn't believe in writing.

Collection: price upon request • Catalog: 93 pages, in wrappers, $25

Glenn Horowitz Bookseller

7 West... ...691-9100

info@g... ...owitz.com

 INTRODUCING
THE LINCOLN MOTOR COMPANY

When did luxury lose focus on the individual and start seeing us all as one? When did it swerve from a singular vision and head for the middle road? We're not sure who led this detour, but a new road starts here with the 2013 MKZ by the Lincoln Motor Company. Now with an innovative push-button shift designed to create an elegantly open and very personal interior cabin space. Get to know the MKZ at **Lincoln.com**.

the PARIS

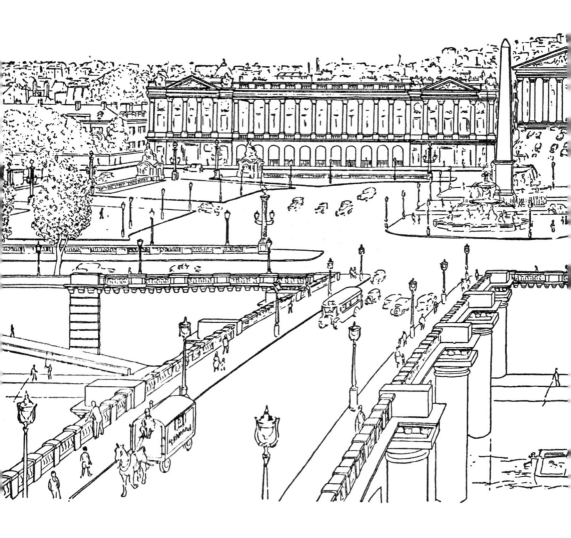

REVIEW

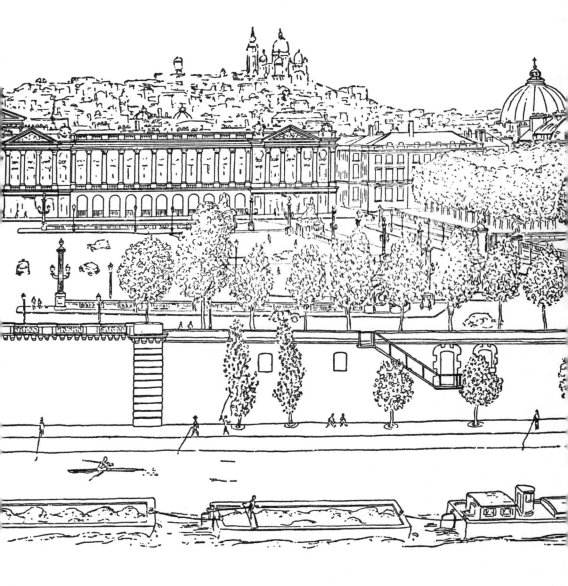

62 WHITE STREET *new york, new york 10013*

rag & bone

NEW YORK

SEIZE *sur* VINGT

MODERN TAILORED CLOTHING

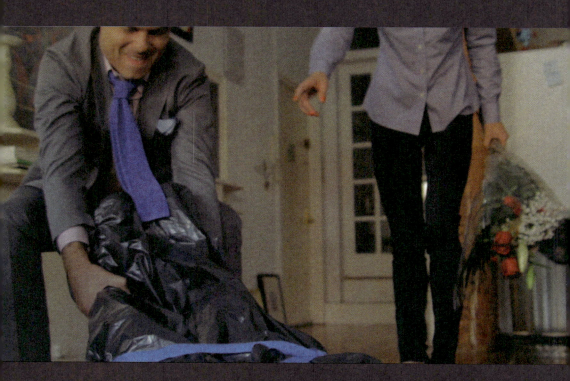

presents

INNES BUTTON

an original story, episodes 1-4 out now

watch on 16sur2o.com and Vimeo

New York   Los Angeles   16sur2o.com

For the cover of our sixtieth-anniversary issue, we asked the French artist JR to make a giant poster of George Plimpton's face and paste it up on a wall in Paris, as a symbolic homecoming and a tribute to the *patrie*. Posters are what JR does. In Vevey, Switzerland, he covered one entire side of a clock tower with Man Ray's *Femme aux cheveux longs*. In Havana, Los Angeles, Shanghai, and Cartagena, Spain, he plastered headshots of elderly residents—headshots many stories tall—across the facades of old buildings. He called the project "The

JR (right) and collaborator, 11th arrondissement, Paris.

Wrinkles of the City." We love these pictures. We love the way they honor the desire behind any portrait—to eternalize a particular face—and at the same time welcome the wear and tear of weather, smog, graffiti: of life as it passes by.

It's been ten years since George died in his sleep, after half a century at the helm of the *Review*. "George," we say, even those members of the staff who never met him. He looms large in our imaginations—as large as that image gazing across the rue Alexandre Dumas—because he invented the form of the *Review* and gave it his spirit. "What we are doing that's new," he explained in a letter to his parents, "is presenting a literary quarterly in which the emphasis is more on fiction than on criticism, the bane of present quarterlies. Also we are brightening up the issue with artwork." This from a man who was about to publish Samuel Beckett! George's magazine was blithely serious and seriously blithe.

One test of a founding editor is whether his magazine can survive him. This was a real question ten years ago, but it was soon answered by George's successor Philip Gourevitch. Since the beginning of Gourevitch's stewardship, the *Review* has grown faster than ever in its history. In the past decade, our circulation has doubled, from the respectable "high four figures" of George's heyday, to nearly twenty thousand. We have won two National Magazine Awards (a prize that always eluded George, to his loud and justifiable chagrin). Then there are the vast and strange domains of the Internet. In the past month alone, our young Web gazette, *The Paris Review Daily*, reached 153,143 readers. Every day more than 270,000 people sample our interviews via Twitter (and every day that number grows). Heaven knows what George would make of these developments—they're puzzling, even to us. Still, we trust he would approve.

In the end, of course, a journal cannot be judged by numbers or awards. It can't be judged by its legacy either. A pedigree means nothing. Over the years, the *Review* has launched hundreds of writers, from Philip Roth and Adrienne Rich to Edward P. Jones and David Foster Wallace, but we are only as good as the issue in your hands. By the time the next one arrives, George's poster will have gone the way of Sitting Bull's; our hope is that his spirit will guide the *Review* as long as there is new writing for us to discover, and artwork to brighten it up.

LORIN STEIN

A year of prizewinning fiction from

RIVERHEAD BOOKS

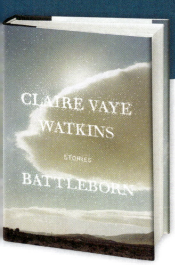

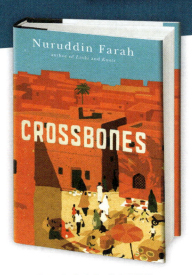

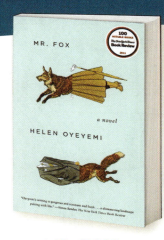

BATTLEBORN
CLAIRE VAYE WATKINS

2013 Story Prize Finalist

CROSSBONES
NURUDDIN FARAH

2012 Hurston/Wright
Legacy Award Finalist

MR. FOX
HELEN OYEYEMI

2012 Hurston/Wright
Legacy Award Finalist

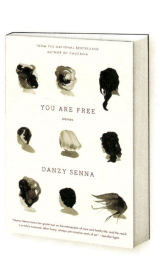

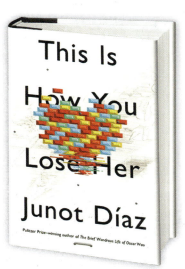

THIS IS HOW YOU
LOSE HER
JUNOT DÍAZ

2012 National Book
Award Finalist

2013 Story Prize Finalist

2012 MacArthur
"Genius" Fellow

YOU ARE FREE
DANZY SENNA

2012 Hurston/Wright
Legacy Award Finalist

Riverhead Books
A Member of Penguin Group (USA) Inc.
penguin.com

J12
CHANEL

TABLE OF CONTENTS

Cover: JR, *Unframed: George Plimpton, 1967*, from a photograph by Henry Grossman.
Frontispiece: William Pène du Bois, *Paris View*.

the PARIS REVIEW

GEORGE PLIMPTON 1927–2003

The Paris Review (ISSN #0031–2037) is published quarterly by The Paris Review Foundation, Inc. at 62 White Street, New York, NY 10013. Vol. 55, No. 204, Spring 2013. Terry McDonell, President; William B. Beekman, Secretary; Lawrence H. Guffey, Treasurer. Please give six weeks notice of change of address. Periodicals postage paid at New York, NY, and at additional mailing offices. Postmaster: please send address changes to The Paris Review, PO Box 23165, Jackson, MS 39225-3165. For subscriptions, please call toll-free: (866) 354-0212. From outside the U.S.: (601) 354-0384 • While The Paris Review welcomes the submission of unsolicited manuscripts, it cannot accept responsibility for their loss or engage in related correspondence. Please send manuscripts with a self-addressed, stamped envelope to The Paris Review, 62 White Street, New York, NY 10013. For additional information, please visit www.theparisreview.org. Printed in the United States. Copyright © 2013 by The Paris Review Foundation, Inc.

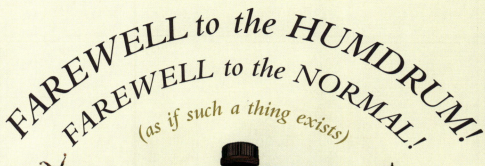

Life is simply too glorious not to experience the odd delights of **HENDRICK'S**® **GIN**, featuring curious yet marvelous infusions of **cucumber** and **rose petal**.

To join our most unusual world visit us at **HENDRICKSGIN.COM**

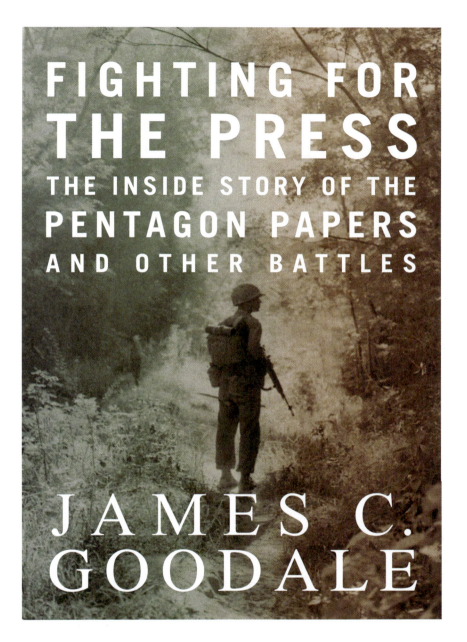

FIGHTING FOR THE PRESS
THE INSIDE STORY OF THE PENTAGON PAPERS AND OTHER BATTLES

JAMES C. GOODALE

"A very important book ...
both enlightening and entertaining."
—HARRY EVANS

The City University of New York
CUNY JOURNALISM PRESS

FORTHCOMING SPRING 2013 FROM CUNY JOURNALISM PRESS | WWW.PRESS.JOURNALISM.CUNY.EDU

WHAT'S NEW FROM

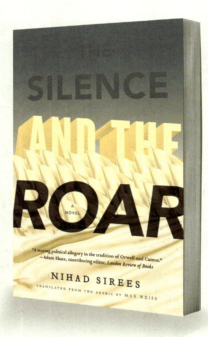

THE SILENCE AND THE ROAR
A novel by Nihad Sirees

"A *1984* for the 21st century...Sirees takes on, with piercing insight, the huge themes of freedom, individuality, integrity, and, yes, love, in this beautiful, funny, and life-affirming novel... *The Silence and the Roar* indisputably connects to current events, but its value as art and political commentary is timeless." —*Publishers Weekly*

"In this short, satiric fable, a formerly famous writer silenced by an authoritarian regime finds himself in a predicament where Kafka meets *Catch-22*." —*Kirkus Reviews*

THE ELIMINATION
A survivor of the Khmer Rouge confronts his past and the commandant of the killing fields

"This is a great text, humble in tone and with universal import." —*Le Monde*

"An exceptional document of Primo Levi's caliber...Rithy Panh's book, through its strength, the starkness of its language, and the depths of its mystery, shows its significance." —*Elle*

"A riveting, intimate look deep inside the machinery of the executioner." —*Kirkus Reviews*

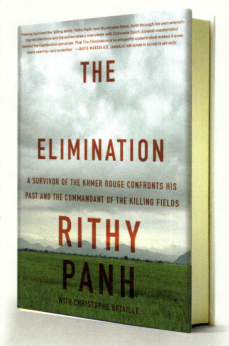

Visit otherpress.com for excerpts and more information

OTHER PRESS

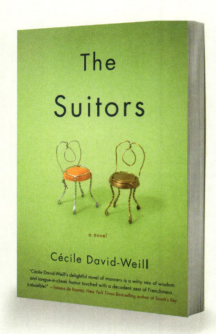

THE SUITORS
A novel by Cécile David-Weill

"A sharply perceptive and addictively amusing insider's look at today's super-rich—a direct heir to Edith Wharton's and Marcel Proust's portrayals."
—Caroline Weber, author of *Queen of Fashion: What Marie-Antoinette Wore to the Revolution*

"A charming peek behind the curtain of French high society as only the ultimate insider can. Cécile David-Weill's novel is a delicious romp and I loved reading it!"
—Ina Garten, *Barefoot Contessa*

WHERE TIGERS ARE AT HOME
A novel by Jean-Marie Blas de Roblès
Winner of the Prix Médicis

"This encyclopedic and mystifying novel, full of picaresque adventures, delights and fascinates…A marvelous, dizzying galaxy, spiraling to the end of the novel." —*Le Figaro littéraire*

"A freewheeling narrative that mixes adventure yarn, magic realism, social comment, political satire, high ideas, popular culture, and a standard injection of sadism and sex." —*Times Literary Supplement*

"Simultaneously channels Umberto Eco, Indiana Jones, and Jorge Amado."
—*Publishers Weekly*

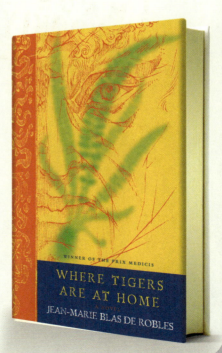

SAPPHIRE · JUSTIN TORRES · JACKSON TAYLOR · AYANA MATHIS · CHRIS ADRIAN

THE **WRITER'S FOUNDRY** MFA

Fall 2013
www.sjcny.edu/mfa

St. Joseph's College
NEW YORK

aperture
210

Hello,
Photography

Photograph by Christopher Williams, 2012 (detail)

The New *Aperture*
Find out more: aperture.org/magazine2013

aperture

Aperture Foundation 547 West 27th Street, 4th Floor, New York, N.Y. 10001
212.505.5555 aperture.org

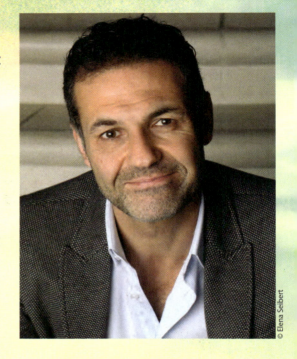
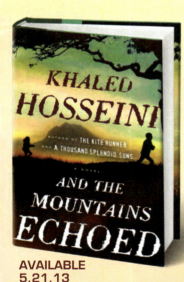

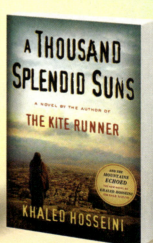

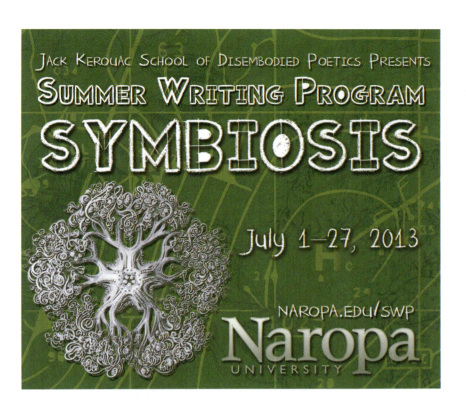
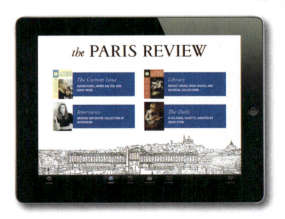

Bettering Myself

—

OTTESSA MOSHFEGH

My classroom was on the first floor, next to the nuns' lounge. I used their bathroom to puke in the mornings. One nun always dusted the toilet seat with talcum powder. Another nun plugged the sink and filled it with water. I never understood the nuns. One was old and the other was young. The young one talked to me sometimes, asked me what I would do for the long weekend, if I'd see my folks over Christmas, and so forth. The old one looked the other way and twisted her robes in her fists when she saw me coming.

My classroom was the school's old library. It was a messy old library room, with books and magazines splayed out all over the place and a whistling radiator and big fogged-up windows overlooking Sixth Street. I put two student desks together to make up my desk at the front of the room, next to the chalkboard. I kept a down-filled sleeping bag in a cardboard box in the back of the room and covered the sleeping bag with old newspapers. Between classes I took the sleeping bag out, locked the door, and napped until the bell rang. I was usually still drunk from the night before. Sometimes I had a drink at lunch at the Indian restaurant around the corner, just to keep me going—sharp wheat ale in a squat, brown bottle. McSorley's was there but I didn't like all that nostalgia. That bar made me roll my eyes. I rarely made my way down to the school cafeteria, but when I did, the principal, Mr. Kishka, would stop me and smile broadly and say, "Here she comes, the vegetarian." I don't know why he thought I was a vegetarian. What I took from the cafeteria were prepackaged digits of cheese, chicken nuggets, and greasy dinner rolls.

I had one student, Angelika, who came and ate her lunch with me in my classroom.

"Miss Mooney," she called me. "I'm having a problem with my mother."

She was one of two girlfriends I had. We talked and talked. I told her that you couldn't get fat from being ejaculated into.

"Wrong, Miss Mooney. The stuff makes you thick in the middle. That's why girls get so thick in the middle. They're sluts."

She had a boyfriend she visited in prison every weekend. Each Monday was a new story about his lawyers, how much she loved him, and so forth. She always had the same face on. It was like she already knew all the answers to her questions.

I had another student who drove me crazy. Popliasti. He was a wiry, blond, acned sophomore with a heavy accent. "Miss Mooney," he'd say, standing up at his desk. "Let me help you with the problem." He'd take the chalk out of my hand and draw a picture of a cock-and-balls on the board. This cock-and-balls became a kind of insignia for the class. It appeared on all their homework, on exams, etched into every desk. I didn't mind it. It made me laugh. But Popliasti and his incessant interruptions, a few times I lost my cool.

"I cannot teach you if you act like animals!" I screamed.

"We cannot learn if you are crazy like this, screaming, with your hair messy," said Popliasti, running around the room, flipping books off window ledges. I could have done without him.

But my seniors were all very respectful. I was in charge of preparing them for the SAT. They came to me with legitimate questions about math and vocabulary, which I had a hard time answering. A few times in calculus, I admitted defeat and spent the hour jabbering on about my life.

"Most people have had anal sex," I told them. "Don't look so surprised."

And, "My boyfriend and I don't use condoms. That's what happens when you trust somebody."

Something about that old library room made Principal Kishka keep his distance. I think he knew if he ever set foot in there, he'd be in charge of cleaning it up and getting rid of me. Most of the books were useless mismatched sets of outdated encyclopedias, Ukrainian bibles, Nancy Drew. I even found some girlie magazines, under an old map of Soviet Russia folded up in a drawer marked SISTER KOSZINSKA. One good thing I found was an old encyclopedia of worms. It was a coverless, fist-thick volume of brittle paper chipped at the corners. I tried to read it between classes when I couldn't sleep. I tucked it into the sleeping bag with me, pried open the binding, let my eyes roll over the small, musty print. Each entry was more unbelievable than the last. There were roundworms and horseshoe worms and worms with two heads and worms with teeth like diamonds and worms as large as house cats, worms that sang like crickets or could disguise themselves as small stones or lilies or could stretch their jaws to accommodate a human baby. What is this trash they're feeding children these days, I thought. I slept and got up and taught algebra and went back into the sleeping bag. I zipped it up over my head. I burrowed deep down and pinched my eyes closed. My head throbbed and my mouth felt like wet paper towels. When the bell rang, I got out and there was Angelika with her brown-bag lunch saying, "Miss Mooney, there's something in my eye and that's why I'm crying."

"Okay," I said. "Close the door."

The floor was black-and-piss-colored checkerboard linoleum. The walls were shiny, cracking, piss-colored walls.

I HAD A BOYFRIEND who was still in college. He wore the same clothes every single day: a blue pair of Dickies and a paper-thin button-down. The shirt was western style with opalescent snaps. You could see his chest hair and nipples through it. I didn't say anything. He had a nice face, but fat ankles and a soft, wrinkly neck. "Lots of girls at school want to date me," he said often. He was studying to be a photographer, which I didn't take seriously at all. I figured he would work in an office after he graduated, would be grateful to have a real job like that, would feel happy and boastful to be employed, a bank account in his name, a suit in his closet, et cetera, et cetera. He was sweet. One time his mother came to visit from South Carolina. He introduced me as his "friend who lives downtown." The mother was horrible. A tall blonde with fake boobs.

"What do you use on your face at night?" is what she asked me when the boyfriend went to the toilet.

I was thirty. I had an ex-husband. I got alimony and had decent health insurance through the Archdiocese of New York. My parents, upstate, sent me care packages full of postage stamps and decaffeinated teas. I called my ex-husband when I was drunk and complained about my job, my apartment, the boyfriend, my students, anything that came to mind. He was remarried already, in Chicago. He did something with law. I never understood his job, and he never explained anything to me.

The boyfriend came and went on weekends. Together we drank wine and whiskey, romantic things I liked. He could handle it. He looked the other way, I guess. But he was one of those idiots about cigarettes.

"How can you smoke like that?" he'd say. "Your mouth tastes like Canadian bacon."

"Ha ha," I said from my side of the bed. I went under the sheets. Half my clothes, books, unopened mail, cups, ashtrays, half my life was stuffed between the mattress and the wall.

"Tell me all about your week," I said to the boyfriend.

"Well Monday I woke up at eleven-thirty A.M.," he'd start. He could go on all day. He was from Chattanooga. He had a nice, soft voice. It had a nice sound to it, like an old radio. I got up and filled a mug with wine and sat on the bed.

"The line at the grocery store was average," he was saying.

Later: "But I don't like Lacan. When people are so incoherent, it means they're arrogant."

"Lazy," I said.

"Yeah."

By the time he was done talking we could go out for dinner. We could get drinks. All I had to do was walk around and sit down and tell him what to order. He took care of me that way. He rarely poked his head into my private life. When he did, I turned into an emotional woman.

"Why don't you quit your job?" he asked. "You can afford it."

"Because I love those kids," I answered. My eyes welled up with tears. "They're all such beautiful people. I just love them." I was drunk.

I bought all my beer from the bodega on the corner of East Tenth and First Avenue. The Egyptians who worked there were all very handsome and complimentary. They gave me free candy—individually wrapped Twizzlers, Pop Rocks. They dropped them into the paper bag and winked. I'd buy two or three forties and a pack of cigarettes on my way home from school each afternoon and go to bed and watch *Married…with Children* and *Sally Jessy Raphael* on my small black-and-white television, drink and smoke and snooze. When it got dark I'd go out again for more forties and, on occasion, food. Around ten P.M. I'd switch to vodka and would pretend to better myself with a book or some kind of music, as though God were checking up on me.

"All good here," I pretended to say. "Just bettering myself, as always."

Or sometimes I went to this one bar on Avenue A. I tried to order drinks that I didn't like so that I would drink them slower. I'd order gin and tonic or gin and soda or a gin martini or Guinness. I'd told the bartender—an old Polish lady—at the beginning, "I don't like talking while I drink, so I may not talk to you."

"Okay," she'd said. "No problem." She was very respectful.

EVERY YEAR, THE KIDS HAD TO TAKE a big exam that let the state know just how badly I was at doing my job. The exams were designed for failure. Even I couldn't pass them.

The other math teacher was a little Filipina who I knew made less money than me for doing the same job and lived in a one-bedroom apartment in Spanish Harlem with three kids and no husband. She had some kind of respiratory disease and a big mole on her nose and wore her blouses buttoned to the throat with ridiculous bows and brooches and lavish plastic pearl necklaces. She was a very devout Catholic. The kids made fun of her for that. They called her the "little Chinese lady." She was a much better math teacher than me, but she had an unfair advantage. She took all the students who were good at math, all the kids who back in the Ukraine had been beaten with sticks and made to learn their multiplication tables, decimal places, exponents, all the tricks of the trade. Whenever anyone talked about the Ukraine, I pictured either a stark, gray forest full of howling black wolves or a trashy bar on a highway full of tired male prostitutes.

My students were all horrible at math. I got stuck with the dummies. Popliasti, worst of all, could barely add two and two. There was no way my kids could ever pass that big exam. When the day came to take the test, the Filipina and I looked at each other like, Who are we kidding? I passed out the tests, had them break the seals, showed them how to fill in the bubbles properly with the right pencils, told them, "Try your best," and then I took the tests home and switched all their answers. No way those dummies would cost me my job.

"Outstanding!" said Mr. Kishka when the results came in. He'd wink and give me the thumbs-up and cross himself and slowly shut the door behind him.

Every year it was the same.

I HAD THIS ONE OTHER GIRLFRIEND, Jessica Hornstein, a homely Jewish girl I'd met in college. Her parents were second cousins. She lived with them on Long Island and took the LIRR into the city some nights to go out with me. She showed up in normal jeans and sneakers and opened her backpack and pulled out cocaine and an ensemble suitable for the cheapest prostitute on the Vegas strip. She got her cocaine from some high-school kid in Bethpage. It was horrible. Probably cut with powdered laundry detergent. And Jessica had wigs of all colors and styles: a neon-blue bob, a long blonde Barbarella-type do, a red perm, a jet-black Japanese one. She had one of those colorless, bug-eyed faces. I always felt like Cleopatra next to Opie when I went out with her. "Going clubbing" was always her request, but I couldn't stand all that. A night under a colored lightbulb over twenty-dollar cocktails, getting hit on by skinny Indian engineers, not dancing, a stamp on the back of my hand I couldn't scrub off. I felt vandalized.

But Jessica Hornstein knew how to "bump and grind." Most evenings she bid me adieu on the arm of some no-face corporate type to show him "the time of his life" back at his condo in Murray Hill or wherever those people lived. Occasionally I took one of the Indians up on his offer, stepped into an unmarked cab to Queens, looked through his medicine cabinet, got some head, and took the subway home at six in the morning just in time to shower, call my ex-husband, and make it to school before the second bell. But mostly I left the club early and got myself on a seat in front of my old Polish lady bartender, Jessica Hornstein be damned. I dipped a finger in my beer and rubbed off my mascara. I looked around at the other women at the bar. Makeup made a girl look so desperate, I thought. People were so dishonest with their clothes and personalities. And then I thought, Who cares? Let them do what they want. It's me I should worry about. Now and then I cried out to my students. I threw my arms in the air. I put my head on my desk. I asked them for help. But what could I expect? They turned around at their desks to talk to one another, put on their headphones, pulled out their books, potato chips, looked out the window, did anything but try to console me.

Oh, okay, there were a few fine times. One day I went to the park and watched a squirrel run up a tree. A cloud flew around in the sky. I sat down on a patch of dry yellow grass and let the sun warm my back. I may have even tried to do a crossword puzzle. Once, I found a twenty-dollar bill in a pair of old jeans. I drank a glass of water. It got to be summer. The days got intolerably long. School let out. The boyfriend graduated and moved back to Tennessee. I bought an air conditioner and paid a kid to carry it down the street and up the stairs to my apartment. Then my ex-husband left a message on my machine: "I'm coming into town," he said. "Let's have lunch, or dinner. We can have drinks. Next week. No big deal," he said. "Talk."

No big deal. I'd see about that. I dried out for a few days, did some calisthenics on the floor of my apartment. I borrowed a vacuum from my neighbor, a middle-aged gay with long, acne-scarred dimples, who eyed me like a worried dog. I took a walk to Broadway and spent some of my money on new clothes, high-heeled shoes, silk panties. I had my makeup done and bought whatever products they suggested. I had my hair cut. I got my nails polished. I took myself out to lunch. I ate a salad for the first time in years. I went to the movies. I called my mom. "I've never felt better," I said. "I'm having a great summer. A great summer holiday." I tidied up my apartment. I filled a vase with bright flowers. Anything good

I could think to do, I did. I was filled with hope. I bought new sheets and towels. I put on some music. "*Bailar*," I said to myself. Look, I'm speaking Spanish. My mind is fixing itself, I thought. Everything is going to be okay.

And then the day came. I went to meet my ex-husband at a fashionable bistro on MacDougal Street where the waitresses wore pretty dresses with white lace–trimmed collars. I got there early and sat at the bar and watched the waitresses move around so gingerly with their round, black trays of colored cocktails and small plates of bread and bowls of olives. A short sommelier came in and out like the conductor of an orchestra. The nuts on the bar were flavored with sage. I lit a cigarette and looked at the clock. I was so early. I ordered a drink. A scotch and soda. "Jesus Christ," I said. I ordered another drink, just scotch this time. I lit another cigarette. A girl sat down next to me. We started talking. She was waiting, too. "Men," she said. "They like to torture us."

"I have no idea what you're talking about," I said, and turned around on my stool.

Then it was eight o'clock and my ex-husband walked in. He spoke to the maître d' and nodded in my direction and followed a girl to a table by the window and just waved me over. I took my drink.

"Thank you for meeting me," he said, removing his jacket.

I lit a cigarette and opened the wine list. My ex cleared his voice but said nothing for a while. Then he did his usual hem and haw about the restaurant, how he'd read about the chef in whatever magazine, how the food on the plane was awful, the hotel, how the city had changed, the menu was interesting, the weather here, the weather there, and so on. "You look tired," he said. "Order whatever you want," he told me, as though I was his niece, some babysitter character.

"I will, thank you," I said.

A waitress came over and told us the specials. My ex charmed her. He was always kinder to the waitress than he was to me. "Oh, thank you. Thank you so much. You're the best. Wow. Wow, wow, wow. Thank you, thank you, thank you."

I made up my mind to order then pretend to go to the bathroom and walk out. I took off my dangly earrings and put them in my purse. I uncrossed my legs. I looked at him. He didn't smile or do anything. He just sat there with his elbows on the table. I missed the boyfriend. He'd been so easy. He'd been very respectful.

"And how's Vivian?" I asked.

"She's fine. She got a promotion, busy. She's okay. Sends her regards."

"I'm sure. Send her my regards, too."

"I'll tell her."

"Thanks," I said.

"You're welcome," he said.

The waitress came back with another drink and took our order. I ordered a bottle of wine. I thought, I'll stay for the wine. The whiskey was wearing off. The waitress went away and my ex got up to use the men's room, and when he got back he asked me to stop calling him.

"No, I think I'll keep calling," I said.

"I'll pay you," he said.

"How much money are we talking?"

He told me.

"Okay," I said. "I'll take the deal."

Our food came. We ate in silence. And then I couldn't eat anymore. I got up. I didn't say anything. I went home. I went back and forth to the bodega. My bank called. I wrote a letter to the Ukrainian Catholic school.

Dear Principal Kishka, I wrote. Thank you for letting me teach at your school. Please throw away the sleeping bag in the cardboard box in the back of my classroom. I have to resign for personal reasons. Just so you know, I've been fudging the state exams. Thanks again. Thank you, thank you, thank you.

THERE WAS A CHURCH attached to the back of the school—a cathedral with great big mosaics of people holding up a finger as though to say, Be quiet. I thought I'd go in there and leave my letter of resignation with one of the priests. Also I wanted a little tenderness, I think, and I imagined the priest putting his hand on my head and calling me something like "my dear," or "my sweet," or "little one." I don't know what I was thinking. "My pet."

I'd been up on bad cocaine and drinking for days. I'd roped a few men back to my apartment and showed them all my belongings, stretched out flesh-colored tights and proposed we take turns hanging each other. Nobody lasted more than a few hours. The letter to Principal Kishka sat on the bedside table. It was time. I checked my reflection in my bathroom mirror before I left the house. I thought I looked pretty normal. That couldn't be possible. I put the last of the stuff up my nose. I put on a baseball cap. I put on some more ChapStick.

On the way to church I stopped at McDonald's for a Diet Coke. I hadn't been around people in weeks. There were whole families sitting down together, sipping on straws, sedate, mulling with their fries like broken horses at hay. A homeless person, man or woman I couldn't tell, had gotten into the trash by the entrance. At least I wasn't completely alone, I thought. It was hot out. I wanted that Diet Coke. But the lines to order made no sense. Most people were huddled in random patterns, gazing up at the menu boards, eyes glazed over, touching their chins, pointing, nodding.

"Are you in line?" I kept asking them. Nobody would answer me.

Finally I just approached a young black boy in a visor behind the counter. I ordered my Diet Coke.

"What size?" he asked me.

He pulled out four cups in ascending order of size. The largest size stood about a foot high off the counter.

"I'll take that one," I said.

This felt like a great occasion. I can't explain it. I felt immediately employed with great power. I plunked my straw in and sucked. It was good. It was the best thing I'd ever tasted. I thought of ordering another one, for when I'd finished that one. But that would be exploitive, I thought. Better let this one have its day. Okay, I thought. One at a time. One Diet Coke at a time. Now off to the priest.

The last time I'd been in that church was for some Catholic holiday. I'd sat in the back and done my best to kneel, cross myself, move my mouth at the Latin sayings, and so forth. I had no idea what any of it meant, but it had some effect on me. It was cold in there. My nipples stood on end, my hands were swollen, my back hurt. I must have stunk of alcohol. I watched the students in their uniforms line up for the Eucharist. The ones who genuflected at the altar did it so deeply, wholly, they broke my heart. Most of the liturgy was in Ukrainian. I saw Popliasti play with the padded bar you knelt on, lifting it up and letting it slam down. There were beautiful stained glass windows, a lot of gold.

But when I got there that day with the letter, the church was locked. I sat down on the damp stone steps and finished my Diet Coke. A shirtless bum walked by.

"Pray for rain," he said.

"Okay."

I went to McSorley's and ate a bowl of pickled onions. I tore the letter up. The sun shone on.

Peter Cole

FROM "THE INVENTION OF INFLUENCE"

Precisely this
 afflicts the plagiarist,
or something like
 the X he is:
What's old and has
 long been known,
seems to him new
 and becomes his own.
He's all reception,
 all alone,
and the fruits are manifold
 though the root is one—
thwarted ambition
 and a sense at heart
the doctor describes
 as a kind of cry:
I cannot bear
 not to have been
the first to have uttered
 a certain thing.

An Actor Prepares

DAVID GATES

L ast summer, flying back from Frankfurt, I happened to look up at an overhead screen while trying to learn my lines in *Twelfth Night*, and for a second I thought I saw myself in a promotional video for Singapore Airlines, among a crowd at JFK two weeks earlier. They couldn't possibly have produced such a thing so fast, could they? But there was the distressed-leather jacket, the mirrored sunglasses, the gray hair—silver, let's call it—and the Profile: ah, still a handsome devil. (I was on my way to see a twenty-eight-year-old German woman I'd met in New York, who said if I came over she'd figure out something to tell her boyfriend.) Just this afternoon I told an old friend— someone I've known for years, at any rate—that this was the moment I knew I had to quit acting. I'd studied myself on tape however many hundreds of times, I said, and never had I been so convincing: Who wouldn't cast this guy as the old lech on his last go-round? But of course what bullshit really, that such and such a moment was your little this-was-the-moment-when moment. At the time, I thought it was just a weird thing, which is all it was, and now let's get on with the show.

My father was a film editor—to begin this at the beginning—who'd worked with Stanley Donen and William Wyler, and I really was a handsome devil when I was in my twenties; I might have made it as a B-list male ingenue, saved my money, and lived on a beach the rest of my life. But when I was thirteen, my parents took me on a trip to the East Coast, where we saw Nicol Williamson's *Hamlet* on Broadway, and maybe that was my moment-when moment. My father, to his credit, or not, never tried to talk me out of moving to New York; he even paid for my first year at the Circle in the Square Theatre School. I put in my time as Mortimer Brewster and Professor Harold Hill back in the days when dinner theaters were a thing, and I played Bernardos and Franciscos at this or that Shakespeare festival. One summer I was so broke I took the bus for Massachusetts to work as an "interpreter" at Plimoth Plantation, speaking Pilgrimese ("How are you faring this day?") and affecting puzzlement when tourists—we were to refer to them as "strange visitors"—tried to get me to break character. I'm proud to say that I never appeared in *The Fantasticks*, either on the road or down on Sullivan Street, though I took TV work when I could get it: a blind date in an episode of *Kate & Allie*, and a corrupt lawyer in *Law & Order*. I was understudy to the guy who played A Gent when they brought back *The Cradle Will Rock*; he never missed a night, so I never got to do that first-act number with Patti LuPone. Fifteen years ago, all this amounted to enough of a résumé to get a job at a SUNY branch, teaching what they were pleased to call theater arts; I took the train up to Westchester three mornings a week, a reverse commute among people who seemed to be domestic workers.

Kenny Donnelly was at Circle in the Square at the same time as me, and he always tried to throw work my way. You might have called him a friend too. Last spring I was picking up extra money doing radio commercials while he was finishing a five-month run at Cherry Lane with his adaptation of *The London Merchant; or, the History of George Barnwell*: sort of a *Sweeney Todd* meets *Rocky Horror*, with Rick Calloway—who'd been his partner, off and on, for years—as Sarah Millwood. Kenny had invited me to audition for the murdered uncle, but I'd thought the thing would close in two days.

He comped me for one of the final performances—he was right; the uncle was a great part—and took me out for drinks after. Would I be interested in coming up to Vermont in July? The community theater he'd organized was doing *Twelfth Night* this year, and he needed a couple of professionals to glue it together. Two months in Arcadia: he'd put me up, feed me, and I could have my choice of Orsino or Feste; he'd take whichever I didn't want, and we'd let the amateurs have fun with Malvolio and Sir Andrew and Sir Toby. Barbara Antonelli—I'd worked with Barbara, yes?—was coming up to do Maria, and a Shakespeare professor from the University of Vermont wanted to try Malvolio. For Viola he planned to cast a drama teacher from the local high school; she had a vaguely look-alike brother who was willing to give Sebastian a whirl, although he'd never acted before. And he knew a college girl, a drama major whose father was a lawyer in town, who might be right for Olivia. A good little actress, he thought, quite apart from the fact that the father was on his board.

"I might be getting a little old for Orsino," I said.

"And I'm not?" Kenny said. "Aren't you sweet. Actually, I sort of like the idea of an Orsino who's past his sell-by date. But listen, what you will. As the man says."

I'd booked my trip to Germany for mid-June, but if I made all my connections, I could get to Vermont the day before rehearsals started. Pathetic as it seems, I took the thing seriously and quit getting high in the evenings. I watched Ben Kingsley in the Trevor Nunn film, and listened to whoever it was on the old Caedmon recording. We all know Shakespeare criticism is a rabbit hole, but I bought Marjorie Garber's book, and I found her *Twelfth Night* chapter helpful, if less so than A. C. Bradley's "Feste the Jester," written back in 1929. And I came upon this, from good old Granville-Barker in 1912: "Feste, I feel, is not a young man... There runs through all he says and does that vein of irony by which we may so often mark one of life's self-acknowledged failures. We gather that in those days, for a man of parts without character and with more wit than sense, there was a kindly refuge from the world's struggle as an allowed fool. Nowadays we no longer put them in livery."

The only way I could memorize anymore was to read my scenes aloud, over and over, and I recorded myself so I could listen when I was running or doing errands. The day before I left for Europe, I was walking through

Central Park, yelling along with myself, when I came upon the statue of Hans Christian Andersen, that kindly giant pedophile in bronze, with his open storybook on one knee and a real live little girl on the other, being photographed by her parents: "Fie, thou dishonest Satan!" The daddy picked his daughter up, as I might have picked up a daughter of mine. Even on the plane back from Frankfurt, and then on the train up to Vermont, I kept force-feeding myself Feste, moving my lips as I read and listened. My part of death, no one so true did share it!

I STEPPED OUT ONTO THE PLATFORM in Montpelier as the sun was going down on what must have been a hot day; the last time I'd felt the open air I'd been in Europe. Kenny lifted my suitcases into the trunk of his Saab and drove me through countryside that looked like Germany without the castles. (My little German adventure is a whole other story; but you've seen *The Blue Angel*.) On the way, we passed an Adopt-A-Highway sign with the name of his theater. Kenny told me he'd bought up here when it was still affordable; David Mamet had a house a couple of towns away. "Let it be recorded," he said, "that I loathed the man before he turned Republican. You hungry? I'm a little peckish. Let's go drop in on the folklife."

We stopped at a bar in his town; the kitchen was closed, but the owner, whom Kenny introduced as Mike, went back and started the fry-o-lator to cook us his special wings, while we drank Bud and watched the last innings of a ball game. Kenny got into a discussion with Mike about the Red Sox pitcher ("They're sitting fastball, for Christ's sake—why is he not going to his change?") and bought a round for everybody when the Sox won in the bottom of the ninth.

His house, a big old Vermont cape framed by maple trees, sat on a knoll, up a winding dirt drive. "Hell in the wintertime," he said. He helped me carry my bags to his guest cottage, which had once been the henhouse and still had a wooden cutout of a rooster on the door, with a hand-lettered sign that read NO TEASING. "Aren't you flagrant," I said.

"This is only for my very special guests," he said. "The iron law of country life—don't shit where you sleep."

After he'd made sure the bathroom had soap and sniffed the towels for freshness, we walked up to the top of his hill and looked down at the lights in his six-over-six windows. You could smell the hay that had just been cut in his fields. He pointed up, and what do you know: the Milky Way, with its million million stars. "They used to call that the Pathway of the Secret People," Kenny said.

"Who called it that?" I said.

"I don't know, the ancients? I read it somewhere. Anyhow, that always stuck with me. Yes, hmm, I wonder why. You know, I love this fucking place. I never had a home before. Do I swear like this when I'm sober?"

"It's amazing," I said.

"Yeah, well, those near and dear to us have a different view. You can take the boy out of the city, dot dot dot."

"How is Rick? Is he coming up for this?"

"Oh. You haven't been getting around much. Rick. No, Rick is currently receding at the speed of light. The big bang. Followed by redshift. We are no longer receiving signals from that quadrant. Should I put this in layman's terms?"

"Shit. I'm sorry."

"He always did say this was the ass end of the universe—which one would have thought was high praise, coming from Rick. But I'm not going to start singing that old sweet song. In every other respect, life is very, very good. Life is adverbially good. I own a fucking hill, can you believe that? Your life is going to be adverbially good, I can tell. We're both going through some shit, okay? The key is—Jesus, am I babbling? Come along quietly now, Kenny. Look, I'm a sad old queen and you're a sad old whatever the hell you are. But is life not adverbially good? What say we go down and look at that scene where Malvolio comes in with his yellow stockings—I'm not sure how that's going to play. Given the talent involved. You're not tired, are you? Shit, of course you are. We can do this in the morning."

THE NEXT DAY, KENNY DROVE ME to a first read-through at the theater, a converted barn with seats salvaged from an old movie house. I kissed cheeks with Barbara Antonelli—I hadn't seen her since we'd done *The Crucible* in Williamstown, what, twenty years ago?—then took a seat in the front row. I was waiting for Kenny to get up onstage and do his ladies-and-gentlemen-we're-going-to-have-a-show speech, when a young woman in loose cotton pants came in and sat down, leaving a seat between us, slipped off her sandals, and perched yoga-style, the soles of her feet turned up. The light from the open door caught the side of her face, and you could see the faintest blonde down: Was she beautiful, or only young? She caught me looking, and said, "I'm Julia. I know who you are."

"That makes you special right there," I said. "You're our Olivia, yes? I'm your corrupter of words."

"I know, I've been so looking forward to working with you. I don't really know this play."

"I'm just trusting Kenny," I said.

"Me too, but—can I say something? I don't think he really gets women."

"Well, I could refer you to any number of women who might call my understanding into question."

"Oh yes, he told me you had a history."

"Bless his heart," I said. "He told me you have a future. Then again, he used to say that about me."

"So is this how you charm them all? Pretending like you're old?"

"It's called getting into character."

"I can't decide if I like you or not," she said.

"And does that work for you?" I said. "The frankness thing?"

"If I might interrupt?" Kenny called from the stage. I realized we'd been the only people talking. "We need to get things rolling here. Where's our Viola?"

"In the ladies'," Barbara said.

"Mother of Mercy," Kenny said. "Does anybody else have to go?"

I thought Kenny was a little hard on the schoolteacher who played Viola, a not-especially-boyish-looking lady named Louise. He corrected her lines— "Not 'for what you are.' 'I see you what you are' "—and shot down her idea of giving a sickly smile after her line about Patience on a monument smiling at grief. Bad idea, granted, but of course her real offense was not being Rick Calloway. It seemed to me that Julia would probably be okay. At least somebody had taught her to project, and from the way she carried herself you could see she must have done some dance as well. She played Olivia as bored, spoiled, and flirty—enough like Helena Bonham Carter to make me think she'd rented the video, too. In our first scene, where Feste says, "The lady bade take away the fool; therefore, I say again, take her away," and Olivia says, "Sir, I bade them take away you," she reached over and touched the tip of my nose, and Kenny yelled out, "No, no, no—you're still pissed at him. Again, please?" She looked at me and mouthed, You see? But then she did it over, with just the right pout.

Back at the house, Kenny brought gin, tonic, limes, and a sweating ice bucket out to the screened porch. "A word in your ear?" he said. "I have to live in this town. Not that she's not a lovely girl, but surely you can find other ways of amusing yourself." He dropped a wedge of lime on top of the ice cubes in my glass. "Her parents are good friends."

"I should certainly hope so."

"Please," he said. "Leave the badinage to those of us who know how to do it?" He poured gin. "I would warn you that she drugs a bit, but I know that wouldn't discourage you."

"You're thinking of me back in my glory days." He began pouring gin. "Whoa, easy—when. Exactly what did you tell this young lady about me?"

"Only that you had an eye for the young ladies. And that she might consider resisting your autumnal charms." He topped off my glass with tonic. "Just between you and me and the wall, there's been a little trouble in that quarter."

"Then she needs to rein her in—what's the opposite of autumnal? Vernal?"

"Oh, you're good. She is very gifted."

"So what's this trouble?"

"Well, since you insist on dragging it out of me. One of her professors—I believe he lost his job over it. Her father got all involved in it—not a chappie I'd want to cross. I think he ended up here because of some—well, there I go. He *is* a good friend."

"Just so we're clear," I said, "are you forbidding this or promoting it? Sounds like you've gone out of your way to plant the seed. On both sides."

"Am I that much of a devil?" He began putting ice in his glass. "Not that I mind watching a good train wreck now and again. Just not here." He poured gin, no tonic, and clinked his glass against mine. "Pretty please?"

THE NEXT DAY, I TURNED DOWN Julia's invitation to go swimming after rehearsal, at some locally legendary swimming hole, but that night most of the cast ended up at the bar in the town's Mexican restaurant, owned by the guy Kenny chose to play Sir Toby, who'd had some stage experience, God help us, in a road-company *Joseph and the Amazing Technicolor Dreamcoat.* On Fridays, he provided the entertainment, with mic, stool, and plug-in acoustic guitar, singing what he called sixties and seventies—blessedly, this was a Wednesday. I saw our Sir Andrew, a slender college boy with black-framed glasses, sitting at the end of the bar, beset by Julia, who was touching his upper arm with her fingertips, then her palm, then running the back of her hand down his cheek, then twirling his long hair around her index finger. She saw me watching and gave me her Olivia pout. I took a seat at a table, between Barbara Antonelli and the Viola woman—I've lost her name again—with her supposedly look-alike brother. Louise.

Barbara looked over at the bar. "I'd fight you for her," she said, "but she'll be forty before she knows she's gay. By which time, I'll be dead." I looked to see if Louise had heard, but she was talking with the brother. "How did he drag you up here?"

"I wasn't doing much else," I said. "It's good to see you."

"Don't waste it on me," she said. "He put me up in this dreadful bed-and-breakfast. Who are these people? Could you get me another one? No salt this time. Will we even get through this?"

"One way or another." I looked around for a waitress.

"Aren't you the trouper. Oh, well. A year from now, we'll all be even older. How are you doing? You don't look that much the worse for wear."

"All on the inside," I said.

Louise turned away from talking with her brother. "How do you think I'm doing so far?" she said to Barbara. "Honestly. I'm afraid I'm in over my head."

"Shakespeare," she said. "We're all in over our heads, dear."

"Not you," Louise said. "Or you."

The waitress was standing over us. "You're going to be fine," I said. "Another one of these? No salt? And I'll have a Bud? What can I get you guys?"

"We're good," Louise said. "Have you met Billy?"

"Not officially," Billy said. "You were great this afternoon."

"We'll see when I start having to remember my lines," I said.

"And what is it that you do in real life?" Barbara said to him.

"I was managing a Curves, in St. Johnsbury. We had to close a couple of months ago."

"Curves—now is that a bar?"

"No, you know—Curves. It's like a women's fitness?"

"Oh. Of course. We have those. I was thinking one of those gentlemen's clubs." She turned to me. "When we get back to civilization, let's you and me make an expedition to this one in Midtown—aspiring actresses out the wazoo." She looked over at the bar again; Julia and her young man were gone.

The waitress set down my Bud and Barbara's margarita. "Can I get you folks anything to eat? Marty told me half-price on everything."

"Isn't he a dear," Barbara said. "Can we drink now, think later?"

"Perfect. Kitchen doesn't close till ten."

"And on a weekday night," Barbara said. "I think we should all move up here."

"It's really not such a bad place," Louise said. "The winters can be rough. But I spent a winter in New York once, and that was rough."

"Did you," Barbara said. "Well, then, you know. What about we all settle in Vermont and help Kenny revive the drama."

"Did I hear my name?" Kenny sat down next to me. "They treating you right here?"

"Half-price, can you imagine?" Barbara said. "Anything on the whole menu, from what I could gather. They didn't say about the drinks, though."

"Mother of Mercy," he said. "Okay, I'll take care of this."

"Kenny's a big man in this town," I said.

"I was. You degenerates are ruining my good name." Louise and the brother laughed. Kenny leaned closer to me and said, "Playing a little rough, aren't we?" He stood up. "Let me see if I can awaken our host's bounty."

We dropped Barbara at Blue Jay Way, a Charles Addams house painted San Francisco–style, with a wooden sign out front that showed an officious-looking bird chirping on a twig. I got into the front seat, and Kenny said, "I expect Barbara to be snotty. Believe me, I know how pathetic this must seem to you."

"Come on, you know what my life is," I said. "And everybody here seems to like you."

"And do you hear from Iris?"

"Good Christ," I said. "Why don't you just reach over and slap me like a human being?"

"Well yes, of course, hello, this is the new NPR Vermont—it's now a hate crime not to have David Sedaris on your iPod." There were no other cars out, but he put on his blinker to turn onto the street that led toward his house; only then did I spot a police cruiser with its lights off parked next to the drive-in bank. "Those fuckers," he said. "Pull you over for not having your hands at ten and two. When Rick and I started coming up here, somebody left a dead dog in the mailbox, little miniature poodle or something. Dressed it up in a little pink

T-shirt. I'll never get over it. You know what they said? Call animal control. And then Rick would piss and moan because I kept a shotgun under the bed."

"Jesus. Well, so things are better, no?"

"Any sane person would think so. I mean, even I think so. But I have to tell you, back then they really got who you were. Like: a man who did dirty things to men. So now I'm our oh-so-charming gay theater guy. I mean, who wrote this part? Why am I doing fucking Shakespeare? Why am I not doing Genet?"

"Because Genet is terrible?" I said.

"Well if you're going to be rational about it." He put on his blinker again and took the road that went past a pine-smelling sawmill, lit by a couple of bluish floodlights, then up a steep grade along a rocky stream. "I don't know, I just want to have my nice house on the hill, put on a nice little show for the nice people. This is what it's gotten down to."

"Listen, you're a good man," I said. "I'm going to do my best for you."

"You're a good man," he said. "I think I drank too much again."

"DAILY, AS WE REHEARSE TOGETHER," old Granville-Barker wrote of his production of *Twelfth Night*, "I learn more what it is and should be; the working together of the theater is a fine thing." I just wish you could have seen Julia as Olivia, in the scene where Malvolio comes in with his yellow stockings, and she can't imagine what's gotten into him: she and Kenny worked out this thing where she first had her hands over her mouth, then covered her eyes and watched Malvolio through her fingers, then let out a giggle—just one—despite herself. And meanwhile there was Barbara—always a joy to watch her—trying to keep a straight face as Maria. And even our Malvolio, who'd volunteered because he thought some "acting experience" might help his teaching: Kenny had him worming a finger under his cross-gartering as he said, "And some have greatness thrust upon them." I'm not saying this was magical—I remember what magical was—but I was standing next to Kenny in the wings and I saw him nodding yes.

Julia and Sir Andrew didn't seem to be speaking. A couple of days after their little display at the Mexican restaurant, she and I were out front, watching the scene where he tells Sir Toby, "Your niece will not be seen; or if she be, it's four to one she'll none of me," and he gave us both a look. "Whoa, whoa," Kenny said, "why the stinkeye? Can we keep the fourth wall in place, people?" She put a hand next to my ear and whispered, "He needs to grow up."

The morning of the dress rehearsal, the Eye on the Sky weather forecast was calling for ninety degrees, and we had to set up fans on the stage. I was sweating under my Beckett greatcoat, and I could see Julia was suffering in the long, black mourning dress she had to wear in the first act. The prompter, an English teacher who'd retired from the town's high school, had nodded off by the time we got to the recognition scene; poor Sebastian looked right, looked left—his bewilderment was actually more credible than he'd been able to make it before—then went into improv: "O Viola, is it really thee?" By the time I had to sing "O mistress mine," the guitar I'd borrowed from— now I've lost his name again, you know, Sir Toby—had gone out of tune. "Dress rehearsal is always a disaster," Kenny told us. "Go home, forget about it, and tonight we fucking kill."

JULIA'S PARENTS HAD THE CAST OVER after the performance, to their house across from the village green: your standard-issue New England Federal, three stories, white clapboards, black shutters, oval plaque reading BUILT 1814 beside the front door. In the backyard, they'd strung up chili-pepper lights and set out crudités, earthenware bowls of whitish dips, plastic glasses, a Manhattan skyline of bottles. Malvolio, who'd just promised to be revenged on the whole pack of us, was tapping a microphone while Sir Toby tuned his guitar; they'd been working up a "special" song together. Sebastian, still wearing his soldier jacket with the frogging, was pouring wine for Viola, who'd changed into jeans and a peasant top. No sign of our Sir Andrew. Julia was still in costume, too—the white dress she wore in the last act, cut to make the tops of her pale breasts bulge out—splashing liquor from her glass as she laughed at something with Barbara Antonelli. I started for her, but Kenny touched the back of my arm and brought me over to the mother— a puffy-faced woman my age, whose wooden beads rattled at her tanned bosom when I air-kissed her—then to the father. "Tom," he said, sticking out a hand. "You're quite the actor, aren't you? Even I could see that."

"Didn't I tell you?" Kenny said. "You'll excuse me, I need to go over and pay homage to La Antonelli."

"I shouldn't be admitting this to you," Tom said to me, "but I haven't seen a real Shakespeare since I was at Yale—well no, that's not true, we did see Julia when she was Puck, in sixth grade. Of course, as a father, the leading lady was the whole show."

"I've been very impressed," I said. "Kenny thinks the world of her."

"Well, we all think the world of Kenny. He does a lot for this community—a lot for this family. He won't tell you, but he's the one who got her into Middlebury. He knows one of the muckety-mucks. You'll never hear anybody say a word against Kenny Donnelly."

Julia came over and put an arm around her father. "Kenny says I was naughty." She reached out with the hand holding the glass and touched my nose—as she'd done in our first scene during the performance. (I'd sneaked a look at Kenny in the wings, and saw him throw up his hands.) "I still think it worked."

I saw the father's face get red. "What was this?"

She kissed his fat cheek and said, "Just actor shit. Did you like me?"

"Hey, hey," he said. "Language." She took her arm away and touched my nose again.

"We tend to argue over the fine points," I said, keeping my eyes off the breasts. "I doubt people out there even notice this stuff."

"Don't you have to do what the director tells you?" he said.

"There's always some leeway," I said. "Your daughter's got good instincts."

"Well, I'm sure you know more about it than I do. I thought you were both excellent. You need to go a little easy, Punkin'. Don't forget you got tennis in the morning." He turned away to hug Viola. "Louise, you were terrific. And how about our girl?"

"Is he pissed," she whispered in my ear. "He hates that I'm twenty-one." She finished her drink. "I'm getting more. Come with?"

Malvolio was speaking into the mic. "Is this on? Okay, Marty and I worked up a little number for this occasion…"

"Oh fuck," Julia said. "Let's get away from this."

She took my hand, and as we worked our way to the back door, I heard them singing in unison: "They're gonna put me in the theater…"

We made it into the kitchen, where she shut the screen door behind us, then the wooden door, then leaned her back against it and raised her face.

"Now that you've got me," I said, "what do you plan to do with me?" I went in for the kiss, and she turned her head.

"Make you wait," she said. "Like you did." She flicked her middle finger off her thumb and hit my fly. "I have to get something. Meet me out front, okay?"

"You know, people saw us leave."

She was already starting down the hall that led to the foyer, which had a fanlight above the front door. "We're both twenty-one," she said. "Especially you."

She went upstairs, and I found a bathroom off the hall. I hooked the door behind me and washed my face with cold water. What the fuck are you doing? I said to the mirror. Just the obligatory drunken line: this was as good as done. I waited for her out on the wide stone doorstep and traced the date on the plaque with my index finger, that song from childhood in my head: "Along with Colonel Jackson down the mighty Mississip." She opened the door, still in the dress, thrust a wooden pipe into my mouth and held a lighter over the bowl. Anybody could have seen us from the sidewalk, over the white picket fence. When I exhaled, she kissed me lightly on the lips and said, "Now one more."

"You are crazy," I said.

This time the smoke hit my lungs so sharply I had to cough it out. "Good," she said. "That should do it." We kissed full on: so wide and hard I felt I was biting through into the back of her head. She pulled away, breasts rising and falling. "You're a bastard, you know that? Come."

I followed her to a Lincoln Navigator parked at the curb. "Now where are you taking me?"

"I want to see the famous henhouse. I'll let you pretend I'm one of Kenny's boys. I bet that's what you're really into."

"You have a most inventive mind." My voice sounded far away, and I couldn't remember who Colonel Jackson was. "This is some strong shit," I said.

"Door's unlocked," she said. "You need me to open it for you?"

"I'm fine." This was a car door. It was not beyond me to open it.

I settled in the leather seat, thoughts coming too fast to focus on. She turned on air-conditioning, then music—some kind of music I didn't know how to go about recognizing, except I knew the speakers must be amazing because you couldn't hear down to the bottom. "What is this?" I said.

"Bob Dylan?" she said. And sure enough, it rearranged itself into—what was it? The one about give the bums a dime didn't you, the famous one. "Isn't that your age group? My dad had it in."

"I thought it was an oratorio," I said. A word I didn't know how I knew.

"Wow," she said. "Okay, I want to be where you are."

She pulled over—or had we been moving?—and took her pipe out of the, whatever you call the thing between the seats.

Then we were on some road and the whole inside of the car was flashing blue. "Shit," she said, and the music was gone: big silence. "Just don't say anything, okay?"

Her window was down and a cop was standing there, shining a flashlight. "License, registration?"

"For real?" she said. "We were just out for a drive."

"Yeah, your dad called." He sniffed. "Been smoking that good shit tonight?" He shined the light on the thing between the seats. "What's that? Give it here."

She handed him the pipe.

"What else? Am I going to have to search the car?"

"It's not hers," I said. "I had it."

"Aren't you the gentleman. And you're who?"

"He's in the play," Julia said. "He's a friend of Kenny's."

"I bet he is. See some ID?"

I got my wallet out. "I don't know what you need," I said. "I have this."

He shined his light on my Equity card. "The hell is this, insurance?"

"You can get insurance," I said.

"'Performing for You.' Beautiful. How about a license."

"He lives in New York, for Christ's sake," Julia said. "Nobody drives down there."

"I wouldn't know. So Julia. Do you have any idea why I stopped you tonight?"

"You said. My father called."

"I guess you didn't notice the stop sign back there. How many moving violations have you had in the last year?"

I looked around. We were out in the middle of the country somewhere. Blue flashes kept lighting up a collapsing barn. "Listen," I said. "There's nobody here. Can it be that I was driving?"

"What are you, simple? How did you think it was gonna be?" he said. "Get out of the car."

"You're not gonna hurt him?" Julia said.

He shook his head. "Everything's a drama, right? You got your cell? Why don't you call your folks to come out here, get their car, and drive you home."

"SEE, THAT'S YOUR PROBLEM, you never look on the bright side," Kenny said as he drove me to the train. "You were getting too old to be a matinee idol anyway. Now if they ever bring back *Golden Boy*... Are you hurting? I have some Percocet."

"I fucked up your show," I said. They'd broken my nose when they hand-cuffed me behind my back and shoved my face into the side of the cop car. Kenny came to get me in the morning and told me they were dropping all charges—possession, grand theft auto, resisting arrest—in return for my get-ting out of Vermont. Just a hundred-dollar fine for failure to carry a license.

"Don't give yourself airs," he said. "Rick's coming up. He's going to take over Feste. We'll miss Wednesday and Friday, and then he thinks we'll be ready to roll."

"How did this come about?"

"Pleading? Contrition? I'm an actor, too, don't forget. Actually, I think he was missing me."

"Will he be able to do it?"

"We'll see, won't we?"

"Shit. Maybe I did you a favor."

"One more favor like that and they will run me out of town. You need a keeper."

"Listen, if you know of any."

"Not of your persuasion," he said. "I don't know, I guess not of my per-suasion either." He looked at his watch. "We're way early. I'm still mad at you, by the way. You want to grab a drink?"

YOU'D THINK MY VERMONT ADVENTURE would have put me off the country life, but all this summer I've been renting a small house over-looking a lake in Dutchess County, where you can go out on the deck at night and sit and look up at the Milky Way. Which, yes, you can only do for so long. It was this or get the Profile restored, and I thought I might as well spend the money on myself, if you see what I mean. The trees have already begun to turn; tomorrow I have to give this place up and go back to the city.

Barbara came by this afternoon—she has a cottage in Katonah—and we sat out on the deck in the sunshine. She told me Rick and Kenny were on the outs again, though of course with those two... Anyhow, Kenny was in Chicago for six months, to put together the Lyric Opera's production of *The Balcony*—who knew they'd made that into an opera? *Twelfth Night*, she said, had gone swimmingly. Rick had camped it up as only Rick could do, faked his way through the parts he was sketchy on, and the locals loved him—not to say they hadn't loved me. This was when I told her my little bullshit story.

"I can't hear this," she said. "You're just feeling sorry for yourself. Use it."

"Actually, I'm happy to be out of it all."

She put her glass down. "You are, aren't you. You prick. I always thought you'd go down with the ship. This isn't about our little friend, I trust? You have to come to my gentleman's club. You could still pass for a gentleman if you got your face fixed."

"Just tell me when," I said.

I made sure she got out of the driveway all right—we'd both been drinking the summer's last gin and tonics, and this house sits right on a blind curve—then walked out the sliding doors to the deck again. The gray-painted boards still felt warm under my bare feet, but the air was getting chilly; going to need that jacket. The sun hung just above the trees, soon to turn the lake and sky orange, soon to be gone. And then the stars. You don't imagine, do you, that anyone's watching us, our love scenes and death scenes, and thinking, I see you what you are. But this has nothing to do with anything: I have my clothes to pack for tomorrow, the books I brought, the DVDs, computer, clean the bathroom, wash the last dishes, just a million million little things.

Three Poems by Sylvie Baumgartel

THE MAN IN THE BIG GRAY CAR, PATAGONIA

We began to meet there
On the mops.
After school, during the siesta,
When we could go missing.
No one wonders where you are during the siesta.
Tell me about the women.
What women?
All the women you've been with.
I don't remember, gringa.
Tell me about the ones you do remember.
It's boring.
Bore me.

Tell me about your wife.
Why do you want to know?
What's her name?
Isabella.
Is she beautiful?
Very.
What's her favorite color?
Verde.
Staring at the ceiling,
Talk to me.
Shhhhh.
Talk to me.
Te voy a reventar.

Hector's first love
Was a Mapuche girl.
His parents' laundress.
He would climb

On top of two buckets and
Watch her bathe
By the side of the house.
Purple nipples,
Hair black to her knees.
Who is your impossible love, gringa?
Bill Clinton.
I fall asleep with
My mouth on his arm.

PICNIC WITH MOM

She goes off to look at birds.
I go for a shot in the dark
With room for cream.
I sneeze.
We eat apples
And throw stones into the water.
Westinghouse lightbulbs make us look old.
Westinghouse blender makes us drunk.
I can't build a fire for shit;
I'm not a Girl Scout.
She is tall in wooden shoes.
I am a whore in heels.
I put her braid in my mouth
And bite down hard.

THE FORTUNE TELLER

Lying awake in the middle of the night.
What was and wasn't done.
Things I don't like about people I love.
Origin stories and dress-up.
We look at paintings.
Face of the fortune teller,
Girl who's a thief.
I don't know exactly what I see when I look at you.

I caught you looking at Asian porn—
The pink cavern mouth of a teen
Tied and flayed.
Like Pontormo's Mary,
Eyes of pain and ecstatic same.
You like this, the pain and pleasure in girls.

De La Tour spent his life in Duchy of Lorraine.
Our bed smells of yeast and deer musk.
You woke up and said
You need paintings and champagne.
And to lick a girl with peasant curves.
You've selected me witness
For what was and wasn't done.
I am a thief,
Feed me.

Mad Science

DAVID
SEARCY

I think I need to figure out what I was doing, what I really felt I was up to, as a kid when, overwhelmed by some enthusiasm, some new all-consuming fascination, I'd require it to be fully expressed at once. I'd have to slap together something out of household odds and ends, available parts, to represent whatever it was. And generally leave it at that. Here I only mean the usual sorts of things you would expect to have engaged a dorky child's imagination in the fifties—shortwave radio, rocket ships and outer space, the more spectacular forms of science—and, in the better class of dorky child at least, to have engendered real, immediate, and responsible curiosity, actual seeking after knowledge. I knew kids like that. And admired them all the more to the extent I failed to appreciate that what they really loved were the procedures toward a practical understanding. Strength of character, I preferred to believe, explained it. How they'd plowed through all of that to get to decorate their rooms with apparatus. That the visible instrumentation might be secondary—not sought, nor forced, nor longed for in itself but rather simply coming to be there all around you in your bedroom, easy as anything, as naturally as toys or sports equipment, unself-consciously as that—was a dismaying possibility. It made me wonder sometimes if those kids, smart as they were, knew what all those dials and lights and switches, curly wires and metal rocket parts and laboratory glassware really meant in the overall view of things. One's distant and incapable view of things. Which I may actually have felt permitted insight and perspective unavailable to the competent and concentrated gaze. I may have felt I'd caught a revelatory glimpse of something way out there, the *glint* of all that machinery, the shimmery sense of it, so delicate, thin as paper—cardboard maybe, which is generally what would come to hand when I would try to invoke it with some taped-together cargo-cult construction on my desk. It could be anything. The look was what you wanted. Just the gesture. The idea of dials and switches seemed enough. So, what idea? Enough for what?

What, for example, was I thinking turning my mom's old record player into a seismograph? I mean, my goodness, 78 rpm. That's good for what? For Guy Lombardo. Smart cocktails and fleeting moments. Not the slow, eternal creaking of the Earth. You've seen a seismograph of course, the clocklike turning of the chart against the stylus. It's a meditative instrument. It listens. It has nothing to do with 78 rpm. And I knew that. Yet here I had this thing all set up with a coffee can or something wrapped in graph paper and a brick on top to keep it on the turntable, coat hanger bent around and straining to present a stub of pencil to the chart, and a wire—just plain utility wire—that led from the coat hanger all the way across the room and out a window to a steel rod I had shoved into the ground. And just that crumbly black clay ground that we have here. The kind of ground that grounds things out, where hope and energy go to die, that's not much fun to play in, even. Hard to dig. What information did I think might come from there? What was I thinking? I had read enough to know you needed bedrock. Who had bedrock? Maybe those smart kids. Not me, though. No bedrock here. No fundamentals. Yet it wasn't an altogether empty gesture. You couldn't have it be just that. Once you'd assembled your imaginary instrument, you needed an imaginary quantity, imaginary causes, fainter and fainter suppositions strung together in a Zeno's paradoxical sort of way on out the window to converge upon the vanishing expectation. Say there were out there in the yard, in everyone's yard, the common ground, unlikely properties, effects oblique and subtle and evasive to which bedrock, proper seismographs, and smart kids were insensitive. What if there were vibrations of so high and fine a frequency (the properties of Silly Putty, recently discovered, came to mind) that dirt might act more like a solid or a gel and send its pulse through slack utility wire like wind through weather stripping, mournful saxophones at New Year's. I don't actually remember turning it on. It would have tugged against the weight, the brick and everything on top, to get to speed. And then the coffee can would not have been quite centered, so the pencil would have skipped and dragged and skipped and dragged like time to change the record. And I bet it was a nice day, too. A weekend probably, kids outside, one's whole life out there waiting as I'm standing there and watching this little mark get darker and darker on the pale blue–gridded paper, as if meaning might accumulate or something.

Hank VanWagoner was the most spectacular smart kid in the neighborhood. He lived two or three houses down across the alley, and we'd hear him testing rockets in his backyard sometimes, usually on weekends. Bear in mind, this was before those little foolproof rocket kits came on the market in response to general horror at the mounting number of injuries sustained by young enthusiasts. The call to space rang clear across the land, and none of us who chose to answer was discouraged in the slightest. It was easy for a kid to buy explosives at the drugstore, bring a bag of potassium nitrate home like jelly beans. Though Hank was well beyond such simple, stable, solid fuels and into the truly touchy realm of liquid propellants, which included caustic, toxic, self-igniting hypergolics such as hydrazine and something called "red fuming nitric acid." So we listened, in our own backyards, my parents in their folding canvas lawn chairs, with some interest.

I remember a test so loud it woke me up one Saturday morning, sent me running down the alley. I have no idea where his parents were. I hardly ever saw them, don't recall his mom at all. His sister—rumored to be, in her own way, as precocious as her brother—was an intermittent, dark, alluring presence in the evenings on the balcony outside her little suite above the garage. In any case, Hank seemed to suffer under no constraints and here he was, while other kids were rising to Rice Krispies and cartoons, about to blow it all to hell. A rocket engine, when it's working most efficiently, is pretty close to blowing up. You feel it. You don't have to know a thing to sense some limit is about to be exceeded. It's ecstatic in that way—you grip the Cyclone fence, your face against the wire. You note how close he's standing to it. Is he crazy? There's no smoke, just hard, blue flame and a roar like nothing you're prepared for in the general calm of 1957 or '58 when leaves were raked and airplanes still, for the most part, had propellers. How can he have a thing like that? How can he stand there like he knows what he is doing? It's suspended from a sort of parallelogram that's hinged, I see, to swing up with the thrust, which is recorded by a marker on a graduated chart. All this is clear to me as small details are said to be at the moment of one's death. This sort of noise can only mean that something terrible is happening. Surely everyone can hear it. Surely all the other kids can hear it, paused before their TVs, their Rice Krispies suddenly silent in the bowl. And then the flame is yellow, sputtering, and the parallelogram goes slack, rectangular again. The other noises of the neighborhood return—I can't recall but I imagine barking dogs and screen doors slapping. He had stuff you can't imagine—some sort of rocket-tracking radar thing he showed me once, my God, the dials and switches. And a ten- or twelve-foot framework—maybe six inches in diameter, longitudinal spars and bulkheads made of welded steel and weighing probably fifty pounds—he gave me. The absurdly overbuilt interior structure of some liquid-fueled experiment. Some rocket never launched, I think. Sure, take it. And I did. I dragged it home and leaned it up against the fence, amazed, bewildered like a member of some preindustrial tribe deciding how it might be hammered into spear points. There was nothing to be done with it. My longings seemed to get all tangled up in the rusty pragmatism of it. Here was fundamental structure, to be sure. The wind blew through it. Had we honeysuckle growing on the fence, it would have made a sort of trellis.

Here's what I would do: I'd pack an aluminum tube with about a fifty-fifty mixture of potassium nitrate and sugar—wooden dowel jammed in at one end and a Testors model-airplane enamel screw cap with a quarter-inch hole surrounded by a bunch of little holes because it looked cool at the other—glue three cardboard fins and a cardboard nose cone on, apply the paint (allover silver with red fin tips), touch it off, and watch it melt. What was I thinking? I mean it. What was this half-assed demonstration all about? I knew you couldn't make a proper rocket nozzle out of a screw cap. I could have told you it would blow right out, the glue and the cardboard fins ignite. The melting—more like wilting—aluminum tube surprised me, though. You see, we do learn from our failures.

Have you ever seen Olivier's film of *Henry V*? How carefully it graduates reality from act to act, unfolds it like a pop-up book from stage and painted scenery to something close to real, although compressed into the conventions and the teetery perspectives of the fifteenth-century miniature. And holds it there. You wait for another jump. For the origamic sets to fall away and the play to charge straight out into the world. And it almost does. The massive chivalry of France comes pretty close to bashing through—you think the churning, swampy earth can't get more real than that, but then the battle's over and you look around and find the rolling distances enclosing all this realistic mayhem are imaginary still. "What is this castle call'd that stands hard by?" A miniaturist, imaginary castle folded into painted hills. It's Agincourt. You think of Krishna's admonition that the battle is a dream—and how you want to ask: How is it, then, one's duty to do battle is not also an illusion? And why is the inconsistency so thrilling? So ecstatic to imagine that we merely represent ourselves. That our going through the motions might be everything.

Sometimes on Saturday mornings when there wasn't something noisier going on, you'd hear a kid named Lefty coming up the street. It wasn't his real name, which was Gilbert, nor even descriptive, I don't think. I guess it was just a name he liked. But you could always hear him coming up the street because he always kicked a can. And it was always pretty early. I imagine opening eyes of sleeping parents. Here he'd come. Way down at the end of the block you'd hear him turn the corner. And remember, cans were heavier then. When kicked they went much farther and produced a clearer note. I felt it counted as a sort of public service. Rise and shine. But bright and early as he was, he was benighted. Seventeen years old, I think he told us once. And very tall. But acting, seeming, more like six. We didn't quite know what to make of him. He'd pass by us Saturday mornings—pass right through us in a way, past even our instincts to make fun—and that was usually all we'd see of him that week. One thing about him we admired, though, was his sidearm. It was a Hubley Colt .45 in a leather holster. And although, at eleven or twelve, we no longer placed toy guns at the top of our list, you had to respect the Hubley Colt .45. It was the fanciest, most desirable cap gun out there. No one else had one—an actual full-size copy of an 1860 Colt with a brass-plated cylinder that functioned and received six realistic-looking bullets, each to be realistically charged with a single cap. You had more firepower, I suppose, with one of the ordinary types that loaded end-less rolls of caps. But that was different. There was no conviction there. No sense of the almost-real about it. Someone loved him. Someone understood that the Hubley .45 was the way to go.

One Saturday morning, Bobo Riefler and I were standing in my drive-way by the street and waiting for Lefty. In the garage I'd put together a sort of laboratory: anything that looked good from my chemistry set; a big glass vat (I'm not sure where that came from) full of water into which had been dissolved whatever chemicals were left in those little square bottles, plus a sprinkling of potassium permanganate—wonderfully explosive when mixed with glycerin (just the one-ounce jar please, thank you, and a pack of Dubble Bubble), though here merely for the vivid, toxic purple—and right next to which I'd set up one of those "traveling arc" devices with its brilliantly ascending and expanding and zapping discharge so beloved of mad scien-tists and which, I had been shown by one of the smart kids, could be made from a discarded neon-sign transformer (half-burned-out ones nevertheless were capable of fifteen thousand volts, produced a two- to three-inch spark, and could be had quite inexpensively); and, finally, kind of gathering all this up in a philosophical sort of way, attaching imprecisely here and there like ivy, coils of wire meant to conduct by faith alone the whole idea, whatever it was, the very spirit of mad science, to a leather football helmet I'd sus-pended over a borrowed canvas lawn chair. I would like to suggest that Lefty was our choice for reasons other than unkind ones. Though we were unkind of course—so, as for that, I'm pretty sure what I was thinking. Yet within that there was something else, I want to say—surprising, not unkind. I don't remember what I told him. But I don't think it was difficult to get him to come with me down the crunchy gravel drive to the garage—a little two-car frame garage, quite dark, not finished out or anything, just studs and plank-ing, garden tools and stacks of cardboard boxes, all the stuff that tends to wind up in garages, with my laboratory over in the corner and the lawn chair by itself out in the middle of the concrete floor. I think what was surprising was how easily and heavily he sat there. How resigned he seemed, I guess.

His six-gun shining—just those holsters cost a fortune. They'd have served the genuine article had anybody had one. So, I'm standing at the switch—and naturally nothing's going to happen; nothing ever really happens—but you never know, it's God's domain, and here it's such a beautiful Saturday morning, all our lives aglow out there, somehow, and glaring through the single open overhead door into the dark garage. And Bobo's finally sort of calmed down, thinking who knows what but waiting. And then after I throw the switch we're all still waiting there for a second or two, all three of us, the zapping of the traveling arc behind us, gazing out into the glare, as if some limit were about to be exceeded.

Stephen Dunn

FEATHERS

If a lone feather fell from the sky,
like a paper plane wafting down
from a tree house where a quiet boy
has been known to hide,
you might think message or perhaps
mischief, not just some midair
molting of a bird.
But what if many feathers fell
from a place seemingly higher
than any boy could ever climb,
beyond the top of Savage Mountain
and obscured by clouds.
What might you think then?
A flock of birds smithereened
by hunters? By a jet?
And let's say the feathers were large
and grayish, some of them bloody,
with signs of tendon and muscle
broken off, would you worry about
a resurgence of enormous raptors
only the air force knew about
and had decided to destroy?
For years now you'd heard rumors
of homeless gods in the vast emptiness.
And if they'd appear in your dreams,
as they sometimes did,
begging to be believed in once again,
you'd feel this icy refusal hardening in you.
And when you woke you'd feel it, too.
Your better self wished to believe
the feathers signaled a parade, an occasion

of a triumph, and what was falling
might be a new kind of confetti.
But what, really, was there to celebrate?
Was the world, as you knew it, simply over,
no more rain or snow? Would there always be
this strange detritus coming down,
covering what used to be the ground?

The Art of Fiction No. 218

DEBORAH EISENBERG

Over the past three decades, Deborah Eisenberg has produced four short-story collections: *Transactions in a Foreign Currency* (1986), *Under the 82nd Airborne* (1992), *All Around Atlantis* (1997), and *Twilight of the Superheroes* (2006). She has also written a play, *Pastorale* (1982), a monograph on the artist Jennifer Bartlett (1994), and criticism, much of it for *The New York Review of Books*. Her preeminence as a short-story writer has been recognized by countless critics and a host of awards, including a DAAD residency, the American Academy of Arts and Letters Award for Literature, many O. Henry prizes, the PEN/Faulkner Award for Fiction, a Lannan Literary Fellowship, and a MacArthur "genius grant."

The adult narrator of Eisenberg's story "All Around Atlantis" recalls, "Yes, I had nightmares—

children do. After all, it takes some time to get used to being alive. And how else, except in the clarity of dreams, are you supposed to see the world all around you that's hidden by the light of day?" Learning how to live is difficult work for Eisenberg's characters. Her first three collections are largely populated by people whose efforts to piece together what things mean are hobbled; they are youths, travelers, immigrants, and people recovering from trauma—abuse, war, the death of a beloved. In her more recent stories, she also writes about outwardly settled people who, although they may live with spouses and own good china, lead provisional existences laden with perplexity. What mystifies her older characters is not so much how life works but that it is passing.

Our interview took place over three fiercely hot summer days, in the Chelsea apartment that Eisenberg shares with her partner, the writer and actor Wallace Shawn. She works in a small, light-swept garret, flanked by gorgeously planted terraces. On her writing table, next to her laptop, she keeps a little painting of a brick wall to remind her of the air-shaft view from a previous apartment.

Eisenberg speaks slowly, pausing often to find exactly the right words, and makes no effort to conceal her strong emotional responses, whether she is moved to laughter or tears. She is physically slight, but, dressed all in black, perched on a faded divan, and set off by the high, white walls of her living room, she has the arresting elegance of an eighteenth-century silhouette portrait.

—*Catherine Steindler*

INTERVIEWER

Am I right that your first story was published when you were almost forty?

EISENBERG

That would be about right. A story called "Flotsam" was the first to be published, though it was not the first to be written. The first story I wrote was called "Days," and I have very little affection for it.

INTERVIEWER

Why?

I find it ingratiating. That's something one has to watch with first-person narrative, that special pleading for an "I" who is automatically in the right, or is even automatically lovable—whom the reader can snuggle up with and whose plight the reader can sniffle over. Because snuggling and sniffling can derail a more complex relationship between the reader and the material.

"Days" is also by far the most autobiographical piece of fiction I've ever written. I avoid using real people, including myself, in my fiction, but that piece started out as nonfiction—an account of going to the local YMCA and trying to run around the little track there as a way to endure the horrible ordeal of stopping smoking.

I had had no idea how deep the addiction went—it had essentially replaced me. I was a human being who had structured herself around the narcotic and the prop, who had melded with the narcotic and the prop. Once the narcotic and prop were no longer available, the human being simply died. I was left in a kind of mourning. I was grief stricken. I had murdered someone, and it was me. But as it turned out, that was the only way to allow a less restricted human being to take shape and live.

INTERVIEWER

In what way was your smoking self different?

EISENBERG

As a smoker, I was very brittle, very inelastic, rather reckless but not in any way adventurous. I could only sort of topple into one situation or another. I couldn't breathe, I couldn't move, I couldn't change, but I was safe—in the sense of being preserved. It was like being embalmed, like being smoked, I suppose.

When I decided to stop smoking, I didn't realize I would be dissolving the glue that held me together. But by the time you think you need to make a decision, that decision has already been made. The person I was leaving behind to die on the road was already half dead. Still, there wasn't anybody ready to take the place of that dying person for quite some time.

INTERVIEWER

Did writing start to take the place of that dying person?

I'm not sure writing started to take *that* place, but I wouldn't have been able to write if I'd been smoking. I don't think of writing as therapeutic, but I don't know how I could have managed the despair if I hadn't started to write then.

INTERVIEWER

Of course art-making isn't therapy, but I often think artists don't need to be quite so loath to admit some relationship between art-making and therapy.

EISENBERG

Well, I understand that reluctance. If you think you're going to be late for a movie and you walk briskly to the theater, it might be good for you, but that's not why you're walking briskly. Writing does change you, and of course it feels good to do things, so you could say writing is de facto therapeutic. But really, one writes to write.

Of course, there are ancillary advantages to writing fiction. You get to leave your body, for instance, so you can have experiences that a person with your physical characteristics couldn't actually have.

I find it endlessly interesting, endlessly funny, the fact that we're rather arbitrarily divided up into these discrete humans and that your physical self, your physical attributes, your moment of history and the place where you were born determine who you are as much as all that indefinable stuff that's inside of you. It seems so ridiculous. Why can't I just buckle on my sword and leap on my horse and go charging through the forests?

But the real fun of writing, for me at least, is the experience of making a set of givens yield. There's an incredibly inflexible set of instruments—our vocabulary, our grammar, the abstract symbols on paper, the limitations of your own powers of expression. You write something down and it's awkward, trivial, artificial, approximate. But with effort you can get it to become a little flexible, a little transparent. You can get it to open up, and expose something lurking there beyond the clumsy thing you first put down. When you add a comma or add or subtract a word, and the thing reacts and changes, it's so exciting that you forget how absolutely terrible writing feels a lot of the time.

INTERVIEWER

In "Days," the narrator, as she withdraws from her addiction, discovers agency and causality. The experience of knowing what she wants and then doing something to make it happen is revelatory for her. It sounds like agency and causality are a part of the pleasure of writing for you.

EISENBERG

Until I stopped smoking, I was committed to inaction. So, yes, the pleasures of making something were new and intense for me when I started writing, and they remain intense.

INTERVIEWER

Many of your female characters are committed to passivity, attached to powerlessness. There's even the little five-year-old in "Mermaids" who comforts herself by imagining her five-year-old male friend tying her up. What do you make of this phenomenon?

EISENBERG

Are women attached to powerlessness, either in reality or in my stories? I don't know. But I do know that women haven't chosen powerlessness for themselves. Powerlessness has been thrust upon them, by other people. In any case, passivity can be very powerful. It's an efficient way of shifting responsibility—and blame—onto other people. And instead of having to do anything, you get to be angry all the time.

INTERVIEWER

What's the pleasure in being angry? It's the most miserable state.

EISENBERG

I'm a bit of an expert on anger, having suffered from it all through my youth, when I was both brunt and font. It's certainly the most miserable state to be in but it's also tremendously gratifying, really—rage feels justified. And it's an excellent substitute for action. Why would you want to sacrifice rage to go about the long, difficult, dreary business of making something more tolerable?

INTERVIEWER

Why was inaction so important to you?

I suppose it was partly personal and partly generational. I came to the sixties early—sometime in the fifties I would say, but you could hear the sixties approaching from afar. And I grew up in a milieu that very much valued accomplishment and credentials. The whole thing made me sick, and I didn't want any part of it, so I cast those values from me. I was fastidious. I wouldn't think of accomplishing a thing or having even one credential—a principled stance that happened to be incredibly convenient for someone paralyzed by terror and confusion.

INTERVIEWER

Your parents cared a great deal about accomplishment?

EISENBERG

Yes. I find that painfully touching, really heartbreaking, to think of now, though I rejected it fiercely then. My parents were the children of Jewish immigrants and ambitiously sought to educate themselves well, to lead an assimilated, middle-class life.

Several generations, really, are required to complete an arrival. My grandparents worked so hard to establish a solid footing in this country for themselves and their children, and my parents continued the endeavor. By the time I came around, I didn't understand the problem at all, although I certainly felt repercussions of the difficulties. My parents were serious people who tried to live correctly, but they were so lacking in self-awareness as to be almost prodigies. I think maybe that's not so unusual among the first generation to be born here. They work so hard to fulfill their parents' hopes for them, to merit the sacrifices their parents made for them and the hardships they went through that they're not allowed to know anything about themselves.

INTERVIEWER

Where did your family come from?

EISENBERG

My mother grew up in Chicago, and my father grew up in a little city called Waukegan, in northern Illinois, that's famous for being the hometown of Jack Benny.

As far as I know, my mother's father was from Belarus. My maternal grandmother purported to come from Saint Petersburg. Did she? I have no idea. I was also told that she came from Kronshtadt. Close enough, I suppose.

At age ten. "I grew up in a milieu that very much valued accomplishment and credentials. The whole thing made me sick, and I didn't want any part of it."

My father's parents were probably from shtetels in Poland or Ukraine or Galicia. Of course, the borders were waving around so much back then you could be born in three places at once. The great cities of the Old World, like Saint Petersburg, Kraków, Vienna, Budapest, acquired a certain mythological function for that group of immigrants. The older my paternal grandmother got, my cousin Katherine tells me, the nearer to Vienna the place of her birth became, until she had been born in Vienna.

I remember once, when I was about five, asking my maternal grandfather, What was it like where you came from? And he said, It was cold. That was the end of the conversation. America was the beginning as far as many of those immigrants were concerned. What happened before that stayed in darkness.

There are certainly bits of my personality that I can't quite account for by my own life history. You know, certain neurotic characteristics, fears. It's a little like wondering why your hair is curly when no one else in your family has curly hair, and it turns out you were adopted.

Those of us who are the grandchildren of immigrants often have a void in our psyche that reflects a situation of danger or terror that our grandparents endured. The first generation born in the United States often tries to erase or suppress what they know of their parents' experience in order to provide a level playing field for their children, but in fact experience and fears can be transmitted in various forms across many generations. Many of us grew up knowing nothing, or next to nothing, about the horrors our grandparents lived through, and when we search for the source of certain anxieties, all we can locate is a kind of blank inscrutability.

INTERVIEWER

You write about that blank inscrutability in "All Around Atlantis," one of a handful of your stories about the Hungarian diaspora. What's your interest in Hungarians?

EISENBERG

For some reason, I fill that inscrutable blankness my forebears left with Budapest. It's a repository for many of my fantasies—superb musicians and writers, splendid cafés, voluptuous pastries.

Among Jewish immigrants to America, there was, at a certain period, a hierarchy of nationalities. My forebears, wherever they were from, were at the bottom of that pile, and the Hungarian Jews were at the apex of that pile.

INTERVIEWER

How did your grandparents establish themselves?

EISENBERG

They did what so many others did. Back then, there was so much more economic mobility and less hostility—or less institutionalized hostility—toward immigrants. My father's father started out as a peddler, and then he had a store that sold all kinds of things. He did very well at it, and he was clever about investments and made a lot of money. He died quite young, just at the onset of the Great Depression, and the money was lost. My mother's parents always lived humbly, but they managed. That grandfather was an extremely talented tailor.

INTERVIEWER

Was your mother educated?

EISENBERG

She got herself educated. She was at the top of her class at a good high school in Chicago. Her older brother—and this was the cause of lifelong bitterness on her part—was sent to college, but she was a girl, and her parents said, Please, how could we afford this? But she went through the University of Chicago on scholarship and graduated Phi Beta Kappa. She was very proud of that. She was, on the one hand, very adventurous, intellectually, and on the other hand, very fearful—she'd always defer to the academic view, to the view of "the authority."

INTERVIEWER

What was she was afraid of?

EISENBERG

I have no idea. But I was the pure expression of her fears.

INTERVIEWER

Do you think she would have been afraid of any daughter? Or were there particular things about you that scared her?

EISENBERG

Both. There she was, trying—with not exactly all of her heart but with a large portion of it—to exemplify acceptability to the world she wanted to be a part of, and there I was, conspicuously the incarnation of her secret strangenesses and unacceptabilities.

From the get-go, I was a catastrophe. When I was two, before I could really talk, I was sent to a Viennese psychiatrist. In Chicago, I mean—not in Vienna. But she really was Viennese. At home, I would grab the phone and yell, *Ja?* just the way Dr. Emmy did.

INTERVIEWER

What did you do to require a psychiatrist?

EISENBERG

I was a juvenile delinquent, I guess. But it was a very lucky thing, actually, because the psychiatrist instructed my parents to send me to a wonderful day school on a little farm. It was run by two lesbian communists, and to this day I just light up with joy when I meet a lesbian communist. The school closed when I was eight, but it gave me a basis, a model of something that still emits faint little beeps of wholesome happiness inside me. It certainly freed me to a great extent from my incredible dependency on my dragon mother.

INTERVIEWER

What was your father like?

EISENBERG

He was a saintly pediatrician, very self-sacrificing, and of course he worked horrifying hours. And my poor mother was dealing with ravaging, chronic back pain. It's awful to live with that and it's terrible for the disposition. There was an atmosphere of anguish, despair, and melancholy in the house. It was alleviated a lot when my brother was around—we were all so happy to see him—but he's older and was away sooner. It's very hard to shake off that atmosphere sometimes, even now.

I have such a great life. I really do. But I always wonder, if I had to live my first twenty-five years over again, would I do it, even if I knew that I would go on to so wonderful a life?

INTERVIEWER

You were twenty-six when you met Wally?

Eisenberg, ca. 1960.

That's right. The Wallace with whom I still live.

Meeting him was a gigantic turning point?

You know, if you woke me up in the middle of the night and asked me, Can another person make someone happy? I'm sure I would shout, No! What a preposterous idea! But my actual life is evidence to the contrary.

That is, happiness isn't like a lollipop that somebody can hand you, but reciprocity can create a lot of space—a sort of playground. Among other things, I very much doubt that I would have had the courage to begin writing if it hadn't been for Wally, who strongly believed that people, including me, should do some work that gives them pleasure, if they have that opportunity.

The impulse to do something as difficult as sit down and write couldn't possibly come from someone else entirely. What do you think it was, in your thirties, that equipped you to want to labor at making a sentence?

Maybe every strange, alienated kid is presumed to write, because people had always said to me, Do you write? And up until I was about fifteen, reading was my great pleasure, and I read a lot. When I was fourteen or fifteen, I always carried a talismanic copy of *Nightwood* or *Against Nature* with me to ward off evil. I'm no longer sure exactly what those books represented to me, but they were very portable. When I was in high school, all my friends said they were going to be writers. And I thought, How come *you* get to be a writer, and I don't? I thought WRITER was written on their foreheads and they saw it when they looked in the mirror, and I sure didn't see it when *I* looked in the mirror.

I always thought of writing as holy. I still do. It's not something to be approached casually.

In the decades when you weren't writing, what were you doing—besides smoking cigarettes?

EISENBERG

I went to a small college in Vermont called Marlboro. I was a terrible student. Toward the end of my second year, I left. With a guy. And we led a life that could be led in the sixties—going here and there, not getting hysterical about making a living, putting this or that in one's mouth and seeing what would happen. You know, the life of the mind, sort of.

Eventually he went to Canada to stay out of Vietnam, and I fetched up—and this was a great stroke of luck—at the New School for Social Research. My mother sent me an ad she'd clipped out of a newspaper, and she said, Anybody can get into this school, and I think you better go to it.

My terror of not having a college degree outweighed my terror of finishing college. It was unthinkable not to—one of those prospects, like getting pregnant, that meant you would just slide off the face of the earth. My parents would pay for school, and I didn't know what else to do. I felt that I'd really come to the end of the line in some way, and frankly, I was quite a wreck.

There was a new program at the New School that offered the second two years of undergraduate study. And they said, Do you want to study the humanities or the social sciences? And I thought, I know what humanities is—it's reading a book. I know how to read a book, so I'll do this other thing.

INTERVIEWER

What was your response to political philosophy?

EISENBERG

It was all kinds of social thought—political theory, economics, some psychology, a little philosophy of history, and so on. When I started, I realized that my classmates had read all of Marx, all of Freud, the neo-Marxists. They knew the Frankfurt School theorists, they had a grasp of history. I knew nothing. There was a whole, large vocabulary involved, a conceptual vocabulary that was completely alien to me. I couldn't comprehend a thing that was said, and my solution to this problem was to stay in bed.

Maybe it was true that anybody could get into that program, but it wasn't so easy to get out! There were two things that were required in order to pass the first year, and one of them was a paper for a certain class. Everybody else chose their subjects early and had written their papers. I showed up to the second-to-last class, and the professor said, Fortunately, there's one paper topic left, which nobody else wanted. So it's yours.

It was on some essays by Theodor Adorno concerning the relationship between sociology and psychology. So I went home with them, and I didn't know whether the book was right side up or upside down. I read those essays more than a thousand times without understanding a word. Then I read them once more, and I understood everything in the whole world.

We also had to take a comprehensive exam at the end of the first year. You had two weeks to pass it, and you had the year's syllabus. Everybody else had been in classes all year, but I had these two weeks. I've always been a very slow reader, but the urgency was great. That exam was one of the best and most exciting things that had happened to me in my whole life. It gave me a kind of foundation.

INTERVIEWER

Foundation for apprehending the world?

EISENBERG

Yes. It was a great school. Hannah Arendt and Hans Morgenthau and Robert Heilbroner and other remarkable people were attached to the graduate faculty then, and undergrads could go to their lectures. I sometimes went, and it was thrilling just to see people who could use their brains like that.

I'd been more or less in a fog my whole life, and here were people for whom it was all in a day's work to identify phenomena, scrutinize them, and apply processes of ratiocination. Not that I sat around reading, say, Heidegger from there on out, but when the time came for me to look at the world, I was a little prepared to do it. I also had some idea of what it meant to learn and how you could go about it.

INTERVIEWER

When you finished school and were living in New York, what was the city like?

It was scrappy. I loved it. But I was very lonely, and I was very confused, and I didn't know what was going to happen to me. I wasn't equipped to do much of anything, and I was too fearful to go out and mix it up in the world, too self-conscious. I didn't think I could do anything. I didn't think I could get a waitressing job—I might as well have been trying to get hired as the head neurosurgeon at Columbia Presbyterian.

INTERVIEWER

Did you manage to get a waitressing job?

EISENBERG

Eventually. Eventually I did this and that, and at a certain point I got together with Wally.

Our first—I guess you'd call it a date—devolved into a passionate argument about Mao. Wally had studied Far Eastern history and was very skeptical about Mao's policies. I knew nothing whatsoever about the question, but I was appalled that someone would so confidently dismiss something that might benefit millions of people. It's funny to think of now, partly because it becomes more and more obvious to me how little people—even people who are supposedly great experts—know about anything. I was completely unaware that we were actually arguing about some abstractions that we were calling "China."

INTERVIEWER

Presumably, your politics have evolved together throughout the years.

EISENBERG

Inevitably one's ideas develop and change, but I've always been ready to oppose. I would say that I was born with the basic sense of politics I have now. Children are in a very weak position, so the question of justice is very alive for many of them. I'm no more alive to matters of social justice now than I was at the age of eight, but of course I know a lot more facts.

INTERVIEWER

Not all children are so attuned to injustice.

I was pampered and very privileged, but I always felt out of place, even scorned. I was not a successful child, and I did not have the rewards of fitting in. It's very difficult to question a system of which you are a beneficiary, but it's easy to question a system of which you are not a beneficiary. So in a way it was almost as natural for me, growing up inside it, to question the validity of the standard middle-class values and beliefs, of cultural assumptions, as it would have been if I had grown up in East Harlem.

INTERVIEWER

Your travels in Central America in the eighties influenced you and Wally quite a bit, did they not?

EISENBERG

Well, after all, we didn't find ourselves there by accident—we *went* there. And we didn't go for a vacation—we went to see what our country was supporting there. We got ourselves equipped with phone numbers of journalists and human-rights workers and so on. We were very aggressive about meeting people who could show us what was going on and introduce us to people there, and we met many, many people who were chasteningly admirable.

Any English speaker can learn a little Spanish, so it was possible to get a real look at what was being done with one's tax dollars—that is, to get a look at how one's tax dollars were being spent to enforce a life of slavery for farmers and to murder people who fought against that. Nothing too unusual, unfortunately, but it's one thing to be familiar with the paradigm and another to see at close range the effects on individuals.

INTERVIEWER

Had anything in your experience prepared you for that?

EISENBERG

I had had an experience when I was seventeen that prepared me a bit for one aspect of traveling between the United States and Central America. One of the students at my boarding school was a boy named Thorsten Horton, and his father, Myles Horton, ran the wonderful Highlander Folk School, which trained labor organizers and civil-rights activists. Rosa Parks was one of the people who had gone there.

Thorsten said to me, and I can still remember his voice saying it, Hey, Eisenberg, do you want to get away from your mother this summer?

Well, the school had been in Monteagle, Tennessee, but the property and land was confiscated by the state. In any case, there was to be a campsite built for Highlander in the Smokies, and did I want to join in? I was allowed to go—I think because my brother was getting married later that summer and my mother wanted me out of the way.

The group consisted of a few young white people, mostly northerners, and a number of young black people from Birmingham, Alabama, where all hell had broken out and people were being subjected to all kinds of brutality. It was a proudly Klan county and we all ended up briefly in jail.

The cops came and awakened us in the middle of the night. First they joked about killing us, but then they said they wanted to make a legal example of us instead, so they took us into jail. I was charged with something called "assimilated intercourse." Very arcane. But eventually it was made clear that I was under eighteen and therefore could not be hanged, so the charge was switched to the other white girl, who was over eighteen, and that part of the case fell apart. Our lawyer was local and, needless to say, astoundingly courageous. This was the summer of 1963, the summer before the three boys—Goodman, Schwerner, and Chaney, the civil-rights activists—were murdered in Mississippi.

But the *shock* came when I returned home. People would say, What was it like, what happened? And when I answered, they would say, No, that's not what it was like, that's not what happened.

So, long before I went to Central America, I was familiar both with the lengths to which people would go in order to evade information and also with the pain of trying to synthesize mutually exclusive realities. The mind simply could not encompass, let alone reconcile, the reality of what we, as a nation, were enacting in Central America and the reality of the heedless, cheerful life that so many people in New York were leading. If one place was reality, the other place could not be reality.

And naturally the most sickening aspect of the disjuncture was the fact that we in the U.S. were benefitting from the violent and wretched world we had fostered in Central America. No degree of outrage would have been sufficient, but in fact there was very little attention directed to the matter at all.

The second time we went to Salvador, we met these absolutely charming young Americans—I think they were Methodists—bringing medicine to areas of violent conflict. They said to us, Why did you come back? You know this situation—you don't have anything more to learn here. And we said, It's just easier, it's more comfortable to be here than to try to live with

With Shawn in New York, 1973. "I very much doubt that I would have had the courage to begin writing if it hadn't been for Wally."

this in New York or even discuss it at a dinner party there. And they said, That's why we're here, too.

In your story "Holy Week," an American travel writer, in order to deal with the disjunction between his American life and the lives he's witnessing in Central America, says, Sure the world is unjust, but we'd be ingrates if we didn't enjoy being on the winning side. His girlfriend doesn't buy that, so she just throws a little guilt-fueled tantrum. Have you found other ways to respond to the knowledge that your nice life and their poverty-stricken ones are not unconnected?

EISENBERG

The way to respond is to be as much of an activist as you can be, in whatever way you can be.

But that's not what I've chosen to spend most of my time on, and naturally, if I'm going to spend my time writing fiction rather than, say, lying down in the path of a proposed tar-sands pipeline, and if I'm going to use my share, or more than my share, of the world's resources to lead this pleasant writer's life, I'm going to want to think there's some value in it—if not in what I myself write, at least in writing in general.

Perhaps I should be more suspicious of my belief that there is inherent value in literature. It could be pure, self-serving, soft-brained romanticism, the belief that probing the most delicate and subtle areas of the mind by, say, listening to music or reading will develop what is human in you. There are abundant examples of reactionary, loony, virulently prejudiced artists and art lovers, so one can hardly insist that art is definitively good for the brain. But I believe that a lack of art is really bad for the brain. Art itself is inherently subversive. It's destabilizing. It undermines, rather than reinforces, what you already know and what you already think. It is the opposite of propaganda. It ventures into distant ambiguities, it dismantles the received in your brain and expands and refines what you can experience.

INTERVIEWER

There's a fair amount of politics in your stories. Do you feel some political purpose when you write?

You know, we've been sitting here, using this word *politics*—but what do we mean by it? Let's say we mean social mechanisms, and systems of social mechanisms, that sort out who gets treated how. Well, every writer—everybody—has implicit views of the way people are related to one another through such systems. And those views are inevitably going to be expressed in a piece of fiction.

And if we mean by *politics* specific events that have occurred in reality, then yes, it's true that my fiction is set in a real, rather than in an invented, world. I, for example, am one of the many writers who portrayed in fiction some of the consequences of the destruction of the World Trade Center. It was a very defining, very altering event, and a shared experience. It would have been highly artificial, and in fact programmatic, to set a story in the United States—particularly in New York—at that time without at least acknowledging it.

Fiction is an excellent way to explore the relationships between people and their contexts. But any real exploration of those relationships is not going to be at all doctrinaire. It's not the purpose or practice of fiction writers to polemicize. On the contrary, fiction might be the most unfettered way to go excavating for evidence of real human behavior and feeling. And if you keep your hands off them, your characters are bound to demonstrate the workings of the world in ways that take you by surprise.

So to answer your question, no, using fiction to support a preexisting idea, about politics or about anything else, is not going to produce something that's valid, and it certainly is not going to produce anything that's interesting. But it's inevitable that your work will express your view of life—and that's desirable.

I used to rant and rail all the time about our national cultural hypocrisy and self-deception—the endless yattering about spreading democracy and our wonderful values and being a model culture, and so on. That just drove me insane. But then as soon as the pictures of torture in Abu Ghraib became public, there was an instantaneous adjustment. There were a couple of weeks of horror, and then we Americans immediately and with great equanimity—even alacrity—exchanged the idea that we were a high-minded and beneficent nation for the idea that we were sadists who tortured people in order to steal their resources.

Well, it turns out I liked it much better the old way, when we were self-deceiving hypocrites. And in retrospect, one can see that although the transition appeared to take only a few weeks, it was being prepared for some years, and by the time it was manifest, we had become very ready to embrace the image of ourselves as ruthless and punitive, as a nation that will assassinate its own citizens, that is willing to kill robotically by drones, that rejects hard-earned instruments of justice, like trials. That is, events that had occurred in the public sphere since 2001 became private events, too, and they were imprinting themselves on our souls in one way or another.

My point is that I wasn't conscious of what I was seeing at the time, and yet that period of transition is what permeates my last collection, *Twilight of the Superheroes*. In fact, obviously, it determined the title. I was living with baffling phenomena and writing stories about other people who were, too.

INTERVIEWER

When you sit down to write, you don't start with a political point or idea. What do you start with?

EISENBERG

I never start with anything.

I once heard Colson Whitehead say that he liked to write fiction because he liked to make things up, and it occurred to me that I *hate* to make things up. Or maybe I like to make things up, but I hate the *feeling* that I'm making something up. Until something I've written has the status of memory to me, it's just not in any way finished. It has to feel as though a totality that was hidden from me is being revealed. The whole thing has to all work at once.

INTERVIEWER

So at a certain moment, near the end of the process, you see it all at once?

EISENBERG

At the very end. I never know whether something is going to work until the last word of the last line of the last draft. Well, to be accurate, it's not the last draft. It's what I think is the last draft. Generally, after I've finished what I think is the last draft, it occurs to me to wonder why I've written the thing in the first place, and then I'm able to write what is really the last draft. But just toward the end of what will turn out to be the penultimate draft, there's a feeling that everything is rushing toward something—turning into an arrow headed at a target.

INTERVIEWER

That must feel fantastic.

EISENBERG

Oh, it does. It takes me a long, long time to write a story. There was a three-year hiatus between my last book and my first subsequent story. I just couldn't do anything of any interest during all that time. So most of the time, it's just maddening to sit there. But there are a couple of great weeks toward the end with each story.

INTERVIEWER

So you hate making things up, but you have to start somewhere. How does that usually work for you?

EISENBERG

I hardly know, myself. I can't explain it, I can't account for it. I don't feel that I have what people mean by an imagination, but when you fall asleep, your dream doesn't start by scratching its head and saying, Oh, no! I can't think of anything to dream!

INTERVIEWER

Do your stories begin in observation?

EISENBERG

I'm incredibly unobservant. I'm always amazed when people notice things and ask questions. Apparently I do take in a certain amount of information, but I don't know where it goes. It certainly doesn't seem to go to my brain.

INTERVIEWER

It only reveals itself to you when you're tinkering with words?

EISENBERG

Exactly. Although sometimes it reveals itself to me when I open my mouth.

I think it's essential to manifest yourself outward somehow. One of the crimes of our time is the way we consolidate resources on people who don't need them rather than educating people—I don't mean indoctrinating people, but educating people, so they can extrapolate their humanity, because that is the pleasure of being alive.

INTERVIEWER

And yet you resisted that pleasure for many years.

EISENBERG

Even now I have a huge resistance to getting to work, perhaps because my body knows how exhausting and shaming it's going to be. I don't want to go through the shame and the exhaustion! I mean this obviously cannot be true for most people who write.

INTERVIEWER

Why not?

EISENBERG

I have friends who are much more fluent, who write much more easily—certainly who write much more copiously. It's infuriating to be so constricted.

INTERVIEWER

How do you overcome your resistance?

EISENBERG

Either you have to quit for good or you have to tough it out. That's the choice. You have to be patient.

INTERVIEWER

And eventually your fingers move?

EISENBERG

Yes, it's like a Ouija board. I write down some little thing, and then eventually something comes out of that, or doesn't. I'm just trying to get down one accurate sentence and then another accurate sentence. And most of my time is spent rearranging the little counters in the sentence. And then the little counters on the page, and then the little counters in the whole.

But there is nothing in my mind when I'm writing until I'm well along in a piece. Until then I have no ideas, no conscious feeling. I'm a person with virtually no feelings.

What do you mean by that? I've seen you laugh and cry and… What do you mean by that?

Oh, that's some other … aspect. Not the aspect of me that writes.

So there you are, dragging along your pencil, and…

You write something and there's no reality to it. You can't inject it with any kind of reality. You have to be patient and keep going, and then, one day, you can feel something signaling to you from the innermost recesses. Like a little person trapped under the rubble of an earthquake. And very, very, very slowly you find your way toward the little bit of living impulse. Of course, many writers manage to condense the process, but things accrue reality through all the millions of unconscious operations that go into writing.

Once you've caught a scent of that little bit of life, what then?

Then I have a big mess on my hands for quite some time. So I ask, What is this and what is this and what is this? I go about things as a hamster would— That's good, I want this little piece of straw. That's bad, get it out of the nest. Somehow I have a feeling, Well, this applies in some way. I may not know how, and I may not know why, but I can tell that here's something connected to something central.

I'm putting this into words, but I never remember when I've finished something how things began to take. But it is a kind of taking, a kind of quickening.

INTERVIEWER

Your stories are so precise, it's hard for me to imagine you don't feel some control of the process.

EISENBERG

I have a feeling of strict control over certain elements. I want the ambiguity of reality, but I don't want any linguistic ambiguity or intellectual ambiguity. To me, an objective is to convey the most ethereal possible experience with the greatest possible clarity. To reach in both directions.

So if something's unclear in the sentence, I'm going to purify it. And I can tell if something's irrelevant. The world is mysterious, everything that happens is mysterious, and you can't begin to approach mystery without absolute crystal clarity. Over the clarity of expression I have control. I make the words as amenable to understanding as I possibly can so that the true mysteries can fill up the pages.

INTERVIEWER

For many of your characters—because they're children or emerging from trauma—the world is especially mysterious. What is familiar to most of us is new to them. What do characters who are ignorant of convention do for you? Why are you drawn to them?

EISENBERG

I think of fiction as a kind of inquiry into what it is to be a human and what it is to be a human now. And my constant task, in my life as well as my writing, is to try to discard layers of obfuscation. If I start out with a character who is somewhat unencumbered by the received, I can start farther along.

Most of the process of writing for me is discarding things. I think, Just get rid of this, just tear it to the ground and start with something more fundamental, vital, and unformulated. Really try to see what's in front of you. I spend most of my time trying to tear away banalities.

There are an infinite number of ways to deceive oneself. You tear down one veil, and you think, Ah, the whole world lies right beyond this. But

Eisenberg in 1997. "I think of fiction as a kind of inquiry into what it is to be a human and what it is to be a human now."

no—there's just another veil and then another veil after that. It's boring and stupid and clichéd, and the thing behind it is also boring and stupid and clichéd. So you try to improve on that and…

INTERVIEWER

By the tenth generation maybe it's not so boring and stupid anymore. This process you describe of peeling back the layers of cliché makes me wonder if you regard writing as a spiritual practice in any way.

EISENBERG

I've never known what is meant by "spiritual." That's a door that seems to be closed to me. When I sit down to work, I'm just trying to get one little thing right. So I suppose in that regard I do consider it a practice. But I don't have more far-reaching goals in mind at all. Just, let's get this little thing right.

But I think what you face when you try to strip away the veils is quite frightening. Because you're disclosing your own impulses, interests, and needs to yourself, and that can be truly sickening. You might find that what passionately interests you is watching a character go to Gristedes and pick up a package of Ring Dings. And you think, I can't really be interested in that. I can't really want to use up a piece of paper on that. But you can't get away from it. The prospect of facing one's own inanity is terrifying.

INTERVIEWER

Is it the terror of one's own inanity, or is it the terror of what's not inane, what is challenging and upsetting?

EISENBERG

Of course one fears that if one turns that tiny key a quarter of a turn in the lock, out will shoot flames and brimstone. But I'm not sure that you can distinguish between your own challenging, upsetting, obliterating demons and your own unchallenging, mundane, obliterating shallowness. When one writes, there's the double horror of discovering not only what it is that one so fears but also the triviality of that fear.

INTERVIEWER

Has writing gotten any less difficult over time?

EISENBERG

When you start writing, your incredulity at the childish, incompetent, graceless thing that you've done is shattering. One of the advantages of having experience as a writer—and there aren't many, in fact I can't think of any other—is that you know you can make the horrible thing better, then you can make it better again, then you make it better again. And you may not be able to make it good, but at least it's not going to be what you're looking at now.

INTERVIEWER

Are there ways in which writing becomes harder with time?

Yes. Most ways. But I don't think it's actually age related, I think it's experience related. For one thing, once you've accomplished a certain thing, it's not available to be done again—you've dispatched it. You have new aspirations to fill the gap, but they're bigger aspirations.

Does writing a novel interest you?

That doesn't seem particularly congenial to me. Apparently, it's my aesthetic to want to make things that are oblique, glancing, ephemeral. Of course, there's a certain—rarely acknowledged but definite—attitude of condescension directed towards short fiction, as if nothing of real importance could be conveyed in less than x number of pages. I've certainly been made to feel that stories are a kiddie form, appropriate to women, as if stories were the equivalent of knitting socks for the men, who are out in the mines, actually *doing* something.

Sometimes I've felt that I should write a novel rather than a story because I'm just so exhausted and the fixed costs for a story are exactly the same as for a novel—you have to contrive a whole world each time. So, after all, it would be easier than writing a collection of stories. But that doesn't seem like a very interesting criterion to me—would it be easier? Even though I complain about the difficulty of writing, I actually don't want it to be easy. I want it to be something that I can't do. I want to be able to do something that I am not able to do.

To be serious, though, writing anything presents its own difficulties and of course writing a novel would feel every bit as insurmountable as writing a collection of stories.

But my stories are getting more complicated, or complex. They encompass more than they used to, because my aspirations have grown.

What are your aspirations?

That's something I can't entirely know. But I do know that I want to make a reader feel something that cannot be put into words, even though that feeling comes out of the words.

The stories of Katherine Mansfield were very important to me when I was a child. My parents owned a book of her stories that had big print and beautiful line drawings, and I thought it was a children's book. The stories were like mist, and I read them over and over. And the magic property of these Katherine Mansfield stories is that when you read them, even as an adult, you think, Now how did the words cause me to have that experience? I've just had an uncanny experience of enormous depth, but I can't see what it has to do with the words.

One of the best things about my adolescence was a movie theater in Chicago called the Clark Theatre. I used to sneak into the city with friends to go there. It showed the great European and Japanese movies, the Italian neorealists and the nouvelle vague and every movie you'd want to see, twenty-four hours a day, seven days a week. I must have seen *Breathless* fifteen times. Watching those movies I realized you could have simultaneous lines—the score, the visuals, the screenplay. It was counterpoint in a narrative form.

INTERVIEWER

Counterpoint?

EISENBERG

I'm just using polyphony as an analogy here. Let's say there are two musical lines, a treble and a bass line, that you're hearing simultaneously. You're experiencing each one, but you're also experiencing what's happening between them. Each line has complete integrity, but the space between them, the harmonic relationship, is just as critical an element, and it's that tension, the way it all works together—that is what is uncannily exciting. How I would love to be able to do something like that! I would love to make some experience for the reader that entails the words and could not be made with other words, but that is much more, and other, than what the words are. And I would love to make some experience that creates all kinds of reverberations between different elements.

Do you think of the thing that happens to a reader as something you control with the words or as something they bring to the words?

On one hand, I'd like to control the experience of the reader very tightly. But on the other hand, I want the reader to be making the experience along with me. And I'm sure that's one reason I have very few readers. A lot of people read to have somebody else tell them exactly what to do with their minds. Not that I don't enjoy reading in that way myself. Right now, I'm reading Trollope's *The Way We Live Now*, which couldn't be more enthralling, but it's nothing other than what it is. Reading it, I'm experiencing the great joy of excellent narrative. But as a writer, I don't have that much interest in narrative. Well, I am interested in narrative, of course, but I like to subordinate it. Or even to pry it out of the piece of paper so it just leaves its tracks—its shape, its motion. For me, a narrative is an expedient to get to something else.

Tell me more about the reader's role.

A piece of fiction is a communication. You're sending an urgent message in a bottle from your desert island. You hope that somebody's going to find the bottle and open it and say, S … O … X? No. S … O …

But the message that is found cannot be exactly the message you've sent. Whatever bunch of words the writer transmits requires a person, a consciousness on the other end, to reassemble it. You know how it feels when you read something that opens up a little sealed envelope in your brain. It's a letter from yourself, but it's been delivered by somebody else, a writer.

Nothing is more fortifying than learning that you have a real reader, a reader who truly responds both accurately and actively. It gives you courage, and you feel, I can crawl out on the branch a little further. It's going to hold.

John Freeman

BEIRUT

That rusting water tower collapsing
on its ruin was the movie theater
where you sat in smoky consternation
while James Bond lit his cigarettes.
This mirrored shopping mall selling
push-up jeans and gleaming watches
used to be the market, where you
could buy za'atar for small change.

Here, on this corner, where your
father explained to a gun in his mouth
that he was driving back to the
apartment to pick up the dog you left
behind. Here is the apartment you gave
to the head of the Deuxième Bureau,
because when such a man asked for a
favor, he did not ask, and you did not say no.

This corner, where the sea shines in the
near distance, is where our friend was shot
through the mouth and wondered, as she
lay, if another bullet would come. Over here,
at that shop where we found the mother-of-
pearl table, is the hotel where snipers played
God and the flies on the corpses in the street
rippled when the fallen were merely
wounded, and still fair game. Here,

where everywhere was somewhere else,
and the street signs point to Paris, and the
light is not to be trusted. It has been so
easily redirected. So we orient through
the night, following the wind, listening for
a sudden noise, waiting for the taste of ashes.

Do You Realize??

———

TESS WHEELWRIGHT

D o you like to go to the club, Mr. Buht?"
the girls drawled coyly, withdrawing
vialed potions and little studded mir-
rors from their purses, unclasping powders, finger-
ing the heavy pendants and charms that clanked
and jangled at their beautiful cleavage—and he
realized, no: he had never been to the club, probably. He couldn't swear he fully knew what one
was. He had been to Bonnaroo; he had pitched his
tent in Big Sur; he had stood with his dogs on the
cliffs of Baja looking out at the bloodred sun sink-
ing into the black of the Pacific, on the long drive
down from Santa Cruz to this teaching post at the
Madison School in Mexico City... But the club,
no, probably not.

He was a very upright sort of American. Not
uptight—he wore his brown hair shaggy; he often
smoked a bowl and then another and pulled Neil

Young up on iTunes, painted a picture or fooled around on his acoustic guitar—but quite without an underbelly. One or both of his two long-haired dogs passed out across his stomach as he watched *O Brother, Where Art Thou?* The world of the elite Mexican adolescents who were his students—who prattled heedlessly as he lectured, and texted under the table, and, in the case of the girls, hit on him more explicitly than fully adult women in his native country ever hit on Ellis Buht—seemed to him intimidating, even nightmarish.

"Open your *Slaughterhouse-Five*, María Cree-stina," he said stiffly. Someone tittered at his pronunciation.

Buht had accepted this job on a whim, via e-mail. Things with a girl back home had cooled; his teacher-trainee contract had been up; something whispered, Dude, the world! Check it out. With the help of his buddy Rook he'd changed all four ball joints and the shocks on his 4Runner—both boys barefoot, with toe rings, dogs underfoot, consulting a MacBook in the grass.

"Bro, you're a force for the good," Buht had announced when they'd finished.

"Bro, ditto!" said Rook, stashing the roach. They embraced briefly and parted. Buht's muscled little mother, dressed always in sweat-absorbent materials and waving five-pound weights, off-loading baggies of macrobiotic snacks, had said cheerful things and wept. His father, a precariously employed advertiser, paunchy and sack-eyed and gentle, thin hair the color of buttermilk long in a fringe behind his ears, waved from the porch of the bunkhouse in back where he'd lived since the divorce six years before. Down Buht had come. "Buht," he told the students, suddenly aware of the fraying hem of his cargo pants. Did they never tread on their hems? "'Byoot'—not 'butt.'"

In many ways initiation had been swift. Quickly, that is, he had understood there would be much he wouldn't understand, and he largely let it be that way. Certain recalibrations were straightforward. For instance, he thought they'd be poor, in the way Americans think Mexicans are poor, but instead they were privileged, in a way Americans can't fully grasp. The students received Lexuses for their fifteenth birthdays; some girls got plastic surgery. They'd been to Japan, to the South of France for the summer holiday; they'd flown quickly up to San Antonio last Saturday for back-to-school shopping. The freshmen *couldn't* get their course syllabi parent initialed—not till October, when the cruise ship docked; overslept seniors flounced in late to class with lipstick-smudged mochaccinos, blaming the driver, the maid.

Of all the kids, it was Juan Miguel Toro—a certain pale-eyed, skinny, earbud-plugged senior of aggressively withheld engagement—who psyched Buht out the most. Buht had been told in his ed. program that it's the kid who psychs you out the most who's the most like you, but Buht felt certain that was not true in this case. Toro liked rap music. Buht thought, and said, that he liked rap music, but he liked the Digable Planets; he liked this albino guy called Doc Francis whom he'd interviewed on his college radio program. This became an area in which Toro planted tests for Buht. "I'm quoting," he'd say, dismissively, in answer to Buht's red pennings beside a line like, "If you think money doesn't grow on trees, you've obviously never sold weed." Juan Miguel spent summers in Miami; Buht had heard him call the math teacher a redneck.

They asked, shuddering, "Mr. Buht, is it horrible downtown?" They asked, "Do you think Gisele Bündchen is classy?" They said, "We think Gisele Bündchen is classy." They said, "Uh, Mr. Buht? There's dog hair on your shirt." When he prompted them to sketch their childhood homes in Personal Memoirs, they asked, "All of them?" When he referred to the tutoring an English-department colleague offered, they said, "Miss Turner is your lover, isn't she?" When he asked them to put away their phones in class, he was told they weren't phones. These were so much more than phones.

The job had come with a list of students who were under no circumstances to be photographed, nor let to linger near the school gates—whereas Buht had believed kidnappers mostly a phenomenon of *Little Orphan Annie*. The school's front walk was lined with bodyguards, radio wires coiling down under their suit collars. Others leered at Buht through the windows of bulky SUVs. "Bway-nos días," he had started off saluting them, to which they patted him down with their eyes. "It takes a while," said Chloe Turner, the tall AP teacher from Connecticut, who always seemed to be smiling a little at her own thoughts. "Qué pasó, Fede?" A stony face at the end of the row softened; the guy nodded to Chloe from behind his shades. She raised her eyebrows at Buht and moved past him toward the school gate. He rehoisted his hemp shoulder bag, reached around to bounce a cargo-pant leg whose hem had gotten underfoot.

Penthouse neighbors got carried off by cops; someone's uncle was in witness protection. A few years back a father had been shot dead, point-blank, with his business partner, while looking at a property in Querétaro.

Estefania Hernández felt she'd been followed from the pharmacy Friday; Adolfo got a weird feeling about his bodyguard and had him traded. "We gave him another raise, but in the end it's a loyalty you can't buy." His soccer buddies nodded knowingly. Buht had played JV soccer. He tried to remember what he and his buddies had talked about. He considered it as he awaited his two noontime quesadillas from the portable outfit up the street, the proprietor of whose son—pop-eyed and shy, an ace whistler, a little fatty—never seemed to go to school at all, but rather kept those two yards of sidewalk impeccable with a big thatch broom. "No onion!" Buht wanted to say, but he'd forgotten how.

Sure, Buht could have studied up more on Mexico before coming down— he'd chatted a bit with the busser at Viva Zapata; he'd bookmarked a URL or two—but anything further wasn't his style. That is, he could tell you a lot about hay-bale construction, about portable solar units, about the breakup of the Beta Band—his was a healthy blog consumption, along its own axes—but he wasn't one to read a formal newspaper too religiously. He considered it his right not to practice, like religion. The reality of his big, aging dog, Chops, and his little, rowdy dog, Flow, seemed nearly always more pressing. The *Santa Cruz Sentinel* never barked to be let out, nor puked in his guitar case.

"Did you come to school in the *metro*, Mr. Butt?" the kids asked knowingly, tittering at this enormous joke.

"Excuse me," said Carlos Rioseco, reassuming his seat after another of the long phone calls he tended to entertain daily in the corridor, smoothing his fine shirt, opened to expose a hairless chest nearly to the navel. (It was Carlos who'd announced during first-day introductions that his stepdad *was* Coca-Cola in Mexico. As a sophomore he'd been cut off in traffic by the same Cadillac Escalade a few funny times one morning and had been pulled then and there for a year of boarding school in Canada.)

"Want me to tell 'em to shut up, Mr. Butt?" offered Jorge Luca, winking at who knows whom, in a spirit Buht couldn't reliably classify. Luca leaned over to whisper something to Rioseco. Buht wondered again if there was something pecuniary in the alliance between these two—the one shouldery, shaved-headed, writing for Personal Memoirs about fights outside the club (he'd broken the jaw of someone who'd called his sister easy, he wrote— telling not showing, vocabulary unvaried, comma-splicing madly—but only because the guy was talking when Luca clocked him: "You can't leave that the jaw to hang loose," he'd written, which Buht had taken to heart); the other pencil-necked and kind of wet looking, a lot of purple in his wardrobe and a length of silk knotted at his throat. A length of silk! Buht himself had gone to a pretty liberal high school, but even there… Clearly the burly gates of acceptance were manned differently down here.

Buht waved them both off now. Where I come from, he protested, silently, feebly, we think you people are poor!

The freshmen cheated. They put their names on sonnets a quick search revealed to be the works of one Doris Morning; they recycled older cousins' papers on *To Kill a Mockingbird*. The time Buht was startled to find, mid-reading quiz, not a crib sheet, not a page of SparkNotes, but the novel itself on one cologne-drenched redhead's lap, the wind had gone out of him. Not that he'd been entirely clean in his day of, say, the odd physics formula inked on the inside lip of his pocket, but this was brazen. At last the cerebral-palsied son of the Chilean ambassador stuttered, "Ugalde him." Of course. Buht came to and sent the cheat to Dean Ugalde.

Buht's seniors, though, were truly subtle. Impressive. Almost heroic, by late week, in their battle against hangovers first period, eyes held open manually, pupils huge and slow, as they hedged bets about Buht's reading questions. At Buht's training school in Santa Cruz, kids slouched, they burped, they pulled their hoods up and over, down to their brows. Here they draped the sleeves of Lacoste sweaters over their shoulders, they pulled chairs out for girls; you sensed their acclimatization to coming home drunk and performing nonetheless a charming round in the dining room, plying a little wit to the high-ranking guest, flattering the aunts, before tilting up the stairs. Eventually they gave up—"Aw, Mr. Buht, it's Friday," shrugging apologetically—and slipped easily and absolutely off task and onto an unabashed rehash of the red-carpet night before: who'd fought and who'd had the blow and how much was he charging; who'd taken whom home and who'd simply taken whom to his car and asked his chauffeur to take a walk; what you could and could not see through Monica Cervantes's baby-pink leggings.

"You should've been there, Mr. Buht," laughed Fofo, in a turtleneck sweater, tossing his slapdash little essay, with Buht's unhappy comments, into the recycle bin as he left. "The freshmen's first party. They called it 'Tequila Mockingbird.'"

Of all kids, it was Juan Miguel Toro whom the others had endowed with a disproportionate authority. Or he'd endowed himself. He was, in any case, the crowned king—the last word, the Law. (It's always someone. In Buht's day it had been the soccer forward, all in all benign. He'd used his centrality largely for good, even—he'd hired Buht's cover band for a party once.) Toro worked over the freshman girls one by one (lovely Alana Sálazar with the big nose and the wonderfully filled-out butt was the most enlightened choice, Buht, in another role, might have judged). Toro sat silent in class with lids half-sunk over red-rimmed eyes—but with none of the mirth of a stoner. He often handed in work with his name in the upper right corner and nothing more on the page. On the day of introductions, when they'd gotten to him, he'd said, "Pass." If he crossed Buht in the hallway he said simply, "Buht," in a commandingly low octave, jutting his chin, as if they were lacrosse team-mates. In the classroom he gave no sign of having seen nor heard Buht.

What Buht needed was a friend. This lack he felt deeply. A friend to help work out the chords of that Petty tune, a friend to prop and pin his bike when the wheel needed truing. A friend with a wheel that needed truing! A friend! Jameson, the Intro Econ teacher, wouldn't serve. He was a bull-necked, tribal-tattooed, former Sigma Pi brother from Milwaukee, danger-ously short, for whom pride issues were chronic. During teachers' Ultimate Frisbee Saturdays, he chased down the tall guys like a boar; twice he'd dived at Ellis Buht, buckling him, and Buht was only of average height. He, like the students, called Chloe Turner's course "Cliterature."

Nor with her had Buht come far toward a friendship. She'd stop by his classroom now and then—he'd grow suddenly self-conscious about the cus-tomized Sublime poster on his wall, the quote from *Ferris Bueller*. It was something about the vintage suit jackets she wore, her height, the words she used, in contexts he wouldn't have thought of: *grotesque, uneven, sexy*.

Plus, Buht quickly deemed her expat findings would have little bearing on his own life:

"Two girls who fuck the same guy are called *hermanas de leche*. What I can't tell is how much hold the Catholic sensibility still has, surreptitiously. I mean among the new wave of bobos. Could be at the end of the day guys are still looking for that doting wife—the Sunday *comida*, the scolding—and you're disqualified if you've 'given it up' too fast. I hate that. Don't beg me, like you have to wear me down. Like, *listen*. Honor my female desire!" It was bothersome to find himself a little hard even as he was trying to remember what *bobo* meant.

"Stop spread-eagling for the gun lobby! Have you put that in your postcards home? We're *sponsoring* this shit show down here, Ellis! Tell your friends in la-la land each time they key a bump of blow they may as well cut a check to Los Zetas."

Spread-eagling? Buht used *fuck* as a swearword. His friends back home preferred drugs they grew themselves. The girls, too, wore windbreakers and said "dude"; they wore colognes of natural oils that smelled like their dinners, and they sang smilingly with bluegrass bands. Didn't Cliterature ever feel like wearing, like, a T-shirt? Her dress was like a rug somehow. He couldn't even tell if she was cute. What was up with a bun right up front like that, like a unicorn? They went for a drink once and he found he had little taste for his beer.

She thought there was necrophilia in *Romeo and Juliet*. She suspected Holden Caulfield desired children. She thought *To Kill a Mockingbird* was a love letter to Harper Lee's father. "And Atticus and Calpurnia are definitely fucking, can we agree?" To this and many other things she said, he had nothing to say back.

(At times Chloe Turner seemed to be proposing sex with him, Ellis Buht, for whom sex was something to be proposed when you truly loved someone, and even then in the most roundabout and noncommittal ways. Ellis Buht still largely approached sex, if he approached sex at all, as if it were something you shouldn't confess you liked. He could, indeed, get a little grumpy with those rare women with whom he'd had it, as if they'd wrested from him and out into the light something kind of grubby, squirrelly, low, which he preferred not to account for in his spirit.)

It was Toro who'd rechristened Women's Lit—like it was Toro who'd fitted Luca and Rioseco out in ski masks and sent them over the school walls one night to leave the shit on Jameson's stack of ungraded midterms. He himself had waited coolly in the get-away Porsche Cayenne. "Pinch-shitters!" Jameson had pretended to laugh it off. As they bore their two-day banishment—from the cameras, Dean Ugalde had matched Luca's Calvin hoodie—Toro sat statue-faced in class as usual. He'd gotten a picture of his testicles on the school Web site, briefly, back in the eighth grade. He'd done coke off Carlos's mom's bible; he'd done coke off the stomach of a college girl. "So then the chick's like, 'Either you really don't like me, or you really want to sleep with me,'" Buht overheard while taking a leak in the student bathroom one recess, "and Toro goes, 'Or both.'"

One Wednesday no one showed up to class. "They're protesting, seems," explained the next-door teacher, a graying gay Aussie who taught listlessly from photocopied worksheets on "Self-Reliance." He sat grading gratefully in the quiet. Gloria Trevi came in low over his computer speakers. "They want lunch lengthened." Buht went to look. Outside, upperclassmen rallied around Toro, who stood with his hands in his pockets, now and then tossing the fringe of blond bangs from his forehead, receiving pounds on the back with just that subtlest thrust of his chin. Jill O'Brien, the principal, stormed across the blacktop, her face red, her awkward coat flapping, looking near tears. By the end of the week, lunch had gotten fifteen minutes longer.

IT WAS FORBIDDEN to sell tickets to the enormous glittery parties it was forbidden to host, and the less sleek kids, the kids without bodyguards, were known to have been suspended for such activity. And yet every Friday there was Juan Miguel Toro peddling tickets by the school buses, holding Buht's eye as he made change.

Sometimes when Buht left the Madison and walked down the hill, the whole basined city seemed engulfed in a thick salmon haze, the jumbled cement homes backing up to the hospital all raw and broken looking, the volcano peeking up through the smog like a great apocalyptic shark fin. Inside the sweaty nine-seater taxi down to Tacubaya, a toddler pointed and stared and clung to his teenage mother, who flicked at the bright plastic tassel bouncing on her cell phone and maybe took a picture. Toro appeared in Buht's dreams: once, they were fighting an old-fashioned duel on the fifty-yard line. Another time, Buht made a move over the desk for his BlackBerry—but it was not a BlackBerry! It was not an iPod Touch. It was an AK-47, which Juan Miguel slowly hoisted, never moving his pale eyes from Buht's forehead.

"HEY, LET ME TALK TO YOU A MINUTE," Buht tried one day as kids filed out after class, in real, waking life, his mouth dry. Buht had been preparing for this. He'd worked up to it. If he couldn't do this, he'd decided, he would give it all up and go home and try to get his old job back, or maybe just stay on his parents' couch and blow on his harmonica. He'd call up his ex and see if she was sure she didn't want to come over and watch DVDs forever.

Toro raised his eyebrows and started out the door.

"I'm worried about you and this course!" Buht called to the boy's back, feeling like his head was in a tin drum.

"Don't worry," Juan Miguel mouthed, laughing, taking the waist of a redhead in volleyball shorts and kneepads, who was leaning against Buht's doorway licking chili off a stick of jicama.

The morning of Model UN, Chloe insisted on buying him a coffee. (Buht had told her about a dozen times he didn't drink coffee, but this she wouldn't accept, which he couldn't help but take as a correctional little warning: *Men* drink coffee.) They slipped from the gym, out the guarded gate ("Buenos días," Buht saluted dutifully; no response) and headed for the café down the street from the school. Seated out front, lo and behold, was Juan Miguel Toro, with an accomplice, baldly skipping opening ceremony, sipping lattes in the sun. If they were ruffled to be caught in defiance of school policy, they gave no sign. Certainly their clothing apologized for nothing: the teenagers were rigged out in light linen suits, shades, the tongues of silk handkerchiefs peeking out their breast pockets, and with what Buht initially would have sworn was a cane, at rest, which turned out on closer inspection to be a leg of a wrought-iron chair, but still. This their spin on diplomat-wear, presumably. The sidekick nodded breezily as the teachers approached. Juanmi didn't even look up.

"Um, but shouldn't you guys be in school?" asked Chloe, looking caught off guard in a way Buht hadn't before seen. She glanced over her shoulder at the school's tall wall; she glanced back at Buht. "H-how did you get off campus?" The gate guards were there to prevent this. Bribing them seemed like too much. But then, looking over the teens now—their watches, their buffed shoes—of course it wasn't.

The sidekick pushed his shades up onto his head. "We've got an inside man," he said. Juanmi smiled slightly. "You're looking very pretty by the way, Miss Turner." Cliterature blushed. Again she glanced at Buht. Her eyes flitted just once to the boys, then dropped to the paving stones. Toro for his part was now staring at her, nakedly. "Let's go," stuttered Chloe at last. Juanmi laughed. Buht raged. Inside he ordered a large black coffee, which he dumped, minus two unhappy sips, into the sink of the boys bathroom back at school.

And when later that morning Buht entered room 204, as supervisor of session 2 of the student WTO, who should be presiding behind the Russia placard, flanked by Jorge Luca and Carlos Rioseco, but fucking Juan Miguel

Toro. They sat smugly in a row at the table under the window. It appeared that during session 1, Russia had won the forgiveness of Georgia and the unprecedented alliance of Brazil—represented, of course, by these same swaggering classmates. A chalked note on the board had been changed to read "10 Minutes: Open Cock-us." The delegate of Portugal, a shy Korean junior, had been told no, Brazil wouldn't be lifting its subsidy on cork, her exports could kiss their trade bloc's ass—and she'd been called the delegate of China. The biology teacher whom Buht was relieving only shrugged as he slipped out.

ONE NIGHT IN WINTER, Buht was leaving a little gathering at the PE teacher's apartment. They'd all watched a basketball game and there had been beer. Chloe had not been in attendance, about which Buht mostly wasn't sorry (a phrase flitted into his head: *Either you really don't like me, or you really want to sleep with me.* Where had he heard that?). In any case, it was one of those nights. In a good way. Finally. He'd almost forgotten these. How 'bout being a fleeting speck on this great gaseous orb? How 'bout plunging ever onward toward the unwritten future? How 'bout the great unsolved mysteries, the vast beyond, the watery depths—the Bermuda Triangle, the North Pole, those people who've trained themselves to hold their breaths for five minutes and follow a guide rope four hundred feet underwater! The Tarahumara, whom the PE teacher had just been telling him about, who run these ultramarathons daily through the canyon beds of the Sierra Madre barefoot! They've been doing it all along; they've never stopped. It didn't seem like too bad a gig. Buht was a little stoned. So *what* if when he listened to Zeppelin's "Tangerine" his heart fell heavily against his ribs with longing for the girl he probably still loved, swelled with the irrational sense that she would walk through the door if he only wished for it hard enough? So what if it maybe always would? "Tangerine" was a hell of a pretty song. That afternoon Buht had watched two little kids playing by a guardrail, the one who could jump it if he used his hands, the one who couldn't. Also they had a battered, paisley suitcase which they wheeled around a little. Their grandmothers or old aunts a bit back on the sidewalk sold razors and batteries and loosies from faded Marlboro packs. One wore an embroidered dress that looked like a sack and the other wore a T-shirt whose stretched letters read LOOKING FOR MR. RIGHT. It was hot and one had pinned her silver braid to the crown of her head with a long bobby pin. Next to them a big, muscled teen sold silly toys—toys that pecked, toys that swam in a little basin of dirty water—very seriously, spitting on the sidewalk. "Hello," said Buht, and all five of them had looked and said, "Hello." How *'bout* that? How 'bout how life had delivered these five and him to the same sun-warm sidewalk this late November afternoon, and they'd exchanged hellos? He felt good about it. He felt good about it! Buht's signature mode, then, at last had caught up with him in Mexico. Maybe next year he'd move to Austin, Texas, and work on farms; maybe he'd go see his old guitar teacher up in Maine and learn scrimshaw. This year would've been this year, and that was something. Buht hailed a cab and got in.

Once within the cab and rolling, the mood changed. Buht had greeted and instructed the driver—not unfluidly, he felt—where he wished to be driven. By midjourney, however, it began to Buht to seem odd that the driver was choosing exclusively dark streets, different than those down which drivers normally drove him. It was very late at night. Buht studied the back of the driver's head. His hair shone, separated into thick slicks like a cow had made them with her tongue; his earlobes hung low, overly fleshy, elephantine; the left one flapped just a little in the stream of wind cutting in from the cracked window. As Buht began to slightly fear this man, even as he told himself there was no reason, he thought of his students. Life might never, ever bring them together. Life might let them dwell in the same earthed-in lake of a metropolitan valley—packed to the former shores with houses cruder by the ring, scores of improvised homes spilling over the foothills and up into the cracks between the mountains, rebar skeletons jutting—and never, ever bring them face-to-face. The way Juan Miguel's family lived, bare-torsoed kids never squirted dubious soapy liquid onto your windshield at red lights, whipping out their wipe rags, implicating you in a transaction before you even sat up straighter; old cripples never leaped to get their oily strips of cast-off shirt onto your shoe as you walked down the street, in the same effort. It all—Buht felt weirdly dizzy, suddenly, even pukey—seemed like a big factor in what was wrong with Juanmi, and this city, and everything.

Meanwhile the cabbie made more unsettling directional choices. Ellis Buht cleared his throat. "Shouldn't, ahem," he began, seeing the guy start just a little. "Shouldn't we take, um, Lázaro Cárdenas?" Later, Buht reflected that this moment, when he started "asking questions," must have started the assailant's heart racing—as when the girlfriend you're preparing to break things off with says, "Is there something you want to talk about?" or when you register and can no longer deny that a kid in the back row is cheating. The authority will ultimately be yours, but the timing never fully is. The driver said something vague, like, "Yeah, no maybe"—absurd. He took a left when where Buht wanted to go was straight.

Buht had been to the Doctores neighborhood once, by day, looking for a part for his truck. Many men had been gathered on a corner, their smeary undershirts rolled up above their hairless bellies, taking turns kind of banging on a car parked there. They had laughed at him. Now there were no such men around, nor anyone. The taxi driver took a left onto a street that was only as empty as the ones they'd been taking but seemed emptier. Where it widened like a river over a field he drifted toward the curb, wrenching around from the driver's seat even as he slowed.

"If you yell, I kill you!" Buht understood only a few beats later, as he understood that the small chunk of metal flashing like a fish in the dimness was a handgun. The guy said it again. It felt exaggerated. If anything Buht had been hooting a little: a ridiculous, unmanly hooting—an approximation of the sound his mother made when water was the wrong temperature, or if he himself as a boy, swimming, had hung onto her in the deep end once he'd gotten too big. In truth his feeling was less of terror and more a kind of "but, but, but!": But I almost didn't get in this cab! I almost didn't go to that dumb party! I almost didn't move to this damn country! There'd been that canoe-trips job . . .

"Your cell phone, little bitchman, give it!"

But, but!—Buht didn't even know what was hitting him. Before he could even decide if he was the kind of guy who fought back (in retrospect, he thought that if he'd set upon that hairy hand with conviction, it could have been overwhelmed, the little gun made to point at, say, the detaching ceiling rug, then wrested away), he did as he was told. He gave over the burlap man-purse he himself had fashioned out of a recycled coffee-bean bag. He emptied his pockets. *Have it all; have my damn phone and all its contacts; they're not real friends, anyway*. His thoughts caught up somewhat, began to place this moment—the weight against his chest of another man, fallen upon him through the space between the seats, groping at his breast pocket, his hips—back into context, into a place between past and future. What had Buht done wrong? What the fuck would he do now? He knew the neighborhood only well enough to know it wasn't one to be left in late at night. It was way more like one to drop off evidence in, to shadow one's vices in general. More conscious of verb conjugation than mugging protocol, he asked if the guy would maybe leave him five pesos to get the bus. "It's that—then I could…" Later, the fact that the guy would not—the fact that the guy would, at this insult of being asked, stick the little gun very close again to Buht's face—it was all very messy, the whole thing: scrambly, unpicturesque. Buht remained aware of things like the wrist bone sprouting hair, the shine of grease at the elbow crease—they became what he fixed upon. How *different* it would have been if the guy had given him his five pesos and pointed him toward the buses. "Brother," Buht might even now be thinking with regard to this guy, "you needed cash bad, so you learned that little act, poor bastard." As it was, he thought simply, Bastard, or even fucker! or even cocksucking motherfucking shitlicker! Often, later, he'd think about his hand drifting up in the night on that dim Condesa corner, hailing that cab, and it never quite seemed like his hand.

AFTER THAT, BUHT WORKED A LOT from work sheets; he sat a lot at his desk, looking at dry rope and carabiners online. Daydreaming of Joshua Tree. This one boy had a bodyguard who actually shadowed him all day long at a short yard's distance, from first bell through JV football. There he would be, looming by the scanner as the boy learned Web design. He would duck after the boy into Ceramics. Some mornings Buht would cross the pair stepping down from an opaque Lexus LX in resentful silence, like the embittered parties of an arranged marriage. On days Buht could only assume the boy too worn down for the social scrimmage of the long lunch recess, he would observe the two side by side on some isolated bench on the far end of the blacktop, under the failing cedar transplant, both lonely figures with their elbows on their thighs, their chins in their hands, the one in a lumpy navy suit, the other in wide, pale jeans and a damp-looking layering of T-shirts, Slayer on top. The irony was that of all the boys, this one—overly tall, pimpled, dewhiskered only as well as the foregoing would allow, pitched slightly to one side, heavy in womanish places, nervous—looked especially, well, *un*valuable. So unslick, so awkwardly teenaged. It can only have heightened the adolescent horror at one's body—the pain of having no other but this stinky, sticky, ill-fitting house, with all its traitorous issuings, sudden hardnesses and wetnesses—that it have such inconveniencing worth to others.

This? Buht could picture him protesting, beholding himself in the mirror, the fish-white belly, the wide, yellow toes: *This* is what requires constant policing?

"If I'd known in high school what I know now!" interrupted Chloe, swooping in in a stiff red dress. Buht hadn't told her about the mugging and was often glad again. "The handsome senior boys who date freshman? Fags! It makes perfect sense. You're in the closet, they're asking questions, what do you do? Date a little kid! They have their pick, way down there on the social food chain, and then with a freshman they won't have to, god forbid, *eat pussy*"—this she said in lowered tones into Buht's left ear—"and if you choose well, your girlfriend's still got the body of a little boy!"

"You know what, just shut up," said Buht.

"What, baby?"

He drew breath. He exhaled.

"Never mind," said Ellis Buht.

"Come make me, sometime," she said, as she left. "I live in La Roma."

"I THINK YOU'LL BE PLEASED with my homework, Mr. Buht," said Gerardo, a freshman grade grubber and two-time loser for class council, whom more than once Buht had counted as probably his best friend at the school. He lingered now after class, feeding papers into plastic sleeves, clipping these into three-ring binders. He folded his scarf; he took a tissue from Buht's box and rubbed at a spot on his shoe. Generally, he hesitated before the indignity of high-school recess.

"I bet I will, Ger," said Buht. He picked up a nice pen off the floor, chucked an abandoned Starbucks cup into the bin. "I know I will, Gerry, my man." God knows there'd be no competition. Everyone else, when Buht had solicited the facts on Shakespeare it had been their homework to research, had worked their smartphones on their knees ("Do you mean: *William Shakespeare*," Google had corrected on a dozen teenage laps)—phones Buht by now had grown too weary to police. When called out, boys trapped them to the underside of desks with their knees, girls slipped them expertly into Ugg boots. Only Gerardo, bless him, had had a little index card, which he'd removed from a plastic sleeve in his three-ring binder. ("During the Plague, William wrote two erotic poems. One was called 'The Rape of Lucrece.' The other I forget.") Buht had darkened the room and cued a movie, taken a seat in the back where he could lay his head against the wall. Zeffirelli's

Romeo and Juliet. When Friar Lawrence explained to Juliet about the death-simulating potion, the young teens called out, "Roofies!" "Viva México," they cried, when Balthazar's horse overtook the dusty donkey carrying the friar's letter to Romeo. "Viva México, right, Mr. Butt, ha-ha-ha?"

Gerardo beamed. He zipped light and dark pens into their respective compartments within his canvas pencil pouch. He refolded his scarf. He reviewed the list of golf courses Buht would be a fool to miss in Mexico. Buht assured him he wouldn't.

Just then, Toro walked by in the hall, glancing in through the reinforced glass that framed the door. Buht pretended not to notice. When he looked in a second time, Buht raised his eyebrows questioningly, but Juan Miguel moved on.

"Was that Juanmi Toro?" Gerardo asked afterward. "He's the richest kid in school. He said he likes to dissolve freshmen in acid."

Later, after Buht had been to the burrito booth out front, there were two tickets to U2, for two weeks later at the Auditorio Nacional, sitting beside his laptop. Buht took them up and moved quickly to the hallway to look. Toro was turning a corner down by the counseling office. Buht jogged to overtake him.

"Juan Miguel, uh," said Buht. He was a little out of breath. "Hey."

"Hey," said Juan Miguel. He tugged the earbuds from his ears by the wires and turned to Buht.

"Hey, did you leave those—?" began Buht.

"Was it mad hard to learn guitar?" asked Juan Miguel at the same time. He shook his fringe from his forehead, hoisted his pants up an inch by the belt, and lifted his eyes to Buht's. Either they were bluer than Buht had ever noticed, or this had never happened before.

"How do *you* know I play the guitar?" asked Buht. This came out in possibly harsher tones than he'd meant. True, Buht had played twice for the class during free write, but he'd been sure that the first time Toro had been sleeping, and the other time cutting.

The kid's brow furrowed; his half-smile dropped away. He fitted a bud back into one ear, looked at his sneakers. When he looked up again his face was harder.

"Hey!" Buht said again, when Juan Miguel turned away. Buht reached out for his shoulder but balked short of contact; his hand dropped back against his cargo pocket. Juanmi turned back slowly. "Uh, did you leave those tickets on my desk?"

The teen looked levelly at the teacher.

"Do you think I did?" he asked back, finally.

"I never *would* have thought that…" said Buht.

"Well, then don't think it."

"Huh, well but…" said Buht.

Toro shook his head once, slightly, laughed once, harshly.

"Listen, go if you want to, Butt. I got 'em free. We all think U2 is gay, so." He turned, decisively this time, and made for the blacktop, tapping the exit sign once as he went.

BUHT WAS IN THE MIDST of a typical evening—lightly stoned, talking to his dog, drifting around on the Internet (How much to rig out his truck with a Thule rack? Is peat moss maybe a better insulator than hay bale in winter? What was the deal with ketamine, which Rook and Jimmy back home were hyping?)—when his phone rang.

"Yo," said Ellis Buht, considering the number. Not Mexico City. Maybe his mom was trying out a new calling card; maybe his aunt was. The flicker of hope that it was somehow his lost lady—she'd changed her mind, she'd had a prescient dream, she was downstairs right now in the yellow light of the taco takeout, putting her brown hair behind her little ear—was tradition, before it was rational, more faith-like than hope-like, barely observable and not fully nameable among his inner phenomena.

"Yo." he said again. "Hola?" It sounded windy on the other end; he would've said it was the sound of cars, trucks, big rigs, or some strange slowed-down buildup on a deep house track.

"Buht, you hear this crying?" broke through a voice in thickly Mexican English, just as Buht had been about to press End. Crying? He didn't hear any crying. After a pause, another voice, clearer, came on the line:

"We don't hurt your nephew if—" The voice cut off; the line hummed and clicked; there was consultation in the background, and a pause following. Buht pushed Flow's head away. The first voice, at a new distance from the receiver, came through next:

"Juan goes home unhurt when you collect forty thousand dollars and deliver. Guard this number. You can call when you got the money. You have twenty-four hours. Forty thousand, U.S. If it's thirty-five, if it's the other day than tomorrow, Juanito never comes home." Wait, Buht *did* hear crying— a kind of seallike yelling, crying in fits—but it sounded fake. Aw, *man*! Suddenly Buht knew.

"Juanito," he repeated with a little snort. "Yeah, nice."

"We have Juan Miguel. He says it's his uncle is in charge. Don't be wrong, Uncle. You have the number?"

Toro, you're a cocksucker, he wanted to say. How the fuck did Juanmi get his number? You're an asshole and a jackass. I *wish* you'd get kidnapped. Instead he said, "I'm not even going to report this one, Toro. I'll only say this: one day you're going to look back and find this stunt way less funny than you do now. Seriously, bro, you need to find another way to stay entertained." He felt pleased enough with his message. His phone rang another time or two, but he simply let it.

He whistled for his other dog, licking dry lips; he took a piss; he got himself a little more stoned, shuffling through his browser windows with the taskbar shortcut. He considered that Wikipedia may be one of the great authors of our time: "Ketamine users may forget their own names, or that they are human, or even what that means." He saved a used Thule rack to his shopping cart on Amazon. He got a virus warning about the track he was downloading. Slowly he forgot what it means to be human and dozed off in his chair.

A KEY IF UNACKNOWLEDGED REASON Ellis Buht had always ignored the patchy advances of Cliterature was because, frankly, he found the clit hard to find. Dammit! This he'd remembered again tonight. "Come, come in me!" she'd gasped theatrically, on top of him, not long before (he'd heard "Juanmi!" for a second, and frozen). But now, wrapped in a weird silk robe with coffee stains on the accordion sleeves, turned away, selecting a song he didn't know from her music library, she seemed ready to be alone. He was hardly sorry. If he could have been sure there wasn't something he was still supposed to do even now, he'd have been above all relieved. The enormity of her bed had made him feel a little lonely; her resolve to use all of it had been a little stressful. Her urgent instructions, her slithering around, pulling him up, pushing him down—it had been disorienting. And only 60 percent in a good way. He lay there missing a certain little sigh particular to his ex—this thing she did with her tongue, like a kitten lapping milk.

Eventually Chloe stubbed out her smoke and crawled onto the bed, staying on all fours for some kind of spine stretch: concave, convex, concave, convex. Buht longed to be far away, doing something as little like sex as possible. Playing Mario Kart, grubbing on the rare Sausage McMuffin he and Rook would indulge in after a really good jam session.

Instead he said, remembering, "Hey, you never gave Toro my number, did you?" Chloe let her arched back sink. "Like, would you have, for something?"

"Your number?" she echoed. She straightened up into a kneel. In the dim light of the obstructed lampshade—oh *there* were his pants—he tried to read her expression. A blush, was that? If so, what kind?

"Toro, your student?" She smiled oddly. She seemed again overly distracted by the ties of her robe, which she twiddled.

"Well?"

"Why would I have given your student your number?" She swallowed visibly.

Buht sighed. "Never mind," he said. When she suggested then that it was late—the hour, she guessed, for Buht to head on home—he swore he'd been just about to, though in truth his wish to be away hadn't concretized into an actual plan.

BUHT HAD JUST QUIETED his kids Friday morning, about to have them freewrite to "Do You Realize??" by the Flaming Lips, something Buht himself often did in his independent life, preferably with a joint burning in his left hand or otherwise nearby—"*Do you realize? that we're floooating in space?*"—when a stricken-looking hall monitor stuck his head in the door.

"Mr. Buht? Ugalde—Dean Ugalde says all teachers should bring their classes to the gym!" The kid hiccuped; his hand was shaking noticeably as he reached for the doorknob. The closest thing to complete silence as can fall over a large group of adolescents had fallen over Buht's. "*Do you REALIZE?! that happiness ... makes you cry?*" Buht resisted the impulse to turn the song up, maybe to drag the appointed suck-up back into the classroom and turn the song way up, to hook it into some speakers, to blare it and deny anyone exit: "*Do YOU REALIZE?!*" Even as he dutifully paused it, instead; as he folded down his laptop lid and nodded as his questioning kids lined up at the door; ushered them out into the hallway, as Randall Kelley was doing with his next door, he had the song in mind. He hummed a little, unsteadily, as his gaggle passed room 113, 115: "*...that everyone you know someday will die.*" The next urge Buht fought was to simply direct his flock leftward, see them merged with the stream of eerily silent students into the gym—there were Cliterature's first-period freshmen, there was Jameson with the Macro kids; he raised his eyebrow at Buht—and he himself make right for the exit gate, hop the first cab home, cue the song to where they'd stopped it in class. "*...and instead of saying all of your good-byes... let them know you re-a-lize...*"

Kids sat on the floor. Teachers sat on the floor. Girls in skirts considered the sneaker skid marks on the court and avoided them and sat on their jackets on the floor. Skinny boys squatted like sidewalk cardplayers. Popular girls sat on bigger, slightly less popular girls' laps. Dean Ugalde and Principal O'Brien stood close together under the far hoop, their coats still on, neither talking nor moving nor looking at anyone. Discipline, drugs! thought Buht willfully. They'd found an eighth in the third-floor bathroom and no one leaves till it's claimed! Someone stole the mascot! It's a Community Day: Ultimate Frisbee and a *taquiza* and we all go home at noon! Ugalde and O'Brien are getting married. Buht felt still other teachers trying to catch his eye, but he avoided contact. Ugalde clipped a mic to O'Brien's collar and she cleared her throat.

The valedictorian got into Harvard! They're gonna film a movie on campus! A dozen juniors cheated on the SAT! "*Do you REALize?! That you have the most beautiful face??!!!*"

"Students, teachers, I have some frightening—some difficult news," said O'Brien, her eyes very wide, her face wet looking under the gym lights. "We want to tell everyone at once. This is very hard. Security is no longer an imminent, that is, an immediate concern, though we know you'll take ... you'll practice ... you'll exercise extra caution." Often Buht had thought she was the most awkward person he'd known. No less now. "One of our senior students, Juan Miguel Toro, was mutila... was injured, was hurt, yesterday evening, last night. There was a crime." No! Buht swung his head this way and that way. He exhaled hotly through his nose like a horse. No, no, *NO!* There was no way! On a recording, the sound that escaped him then could have been a laugh; you could tell by the disturbed way one or two swung to look at him that it read like a laugh. Of all this Buht had very little awareness. His thoughts spun like a hamster wheel; a dark spot condensed in front of his face, then dispersed in zipping beads of light. "He's been recovered ...

that is, he's recovering now, nearby in the Hospital Inglés. It's been precarious … a long night … his condition … the victim…" Buht was dizzy; he spread a hand on the floor in front of him. "I'm sure we'll tell you where you can direct cards, concerns, should you, I know you will… We'll welcome him back, the community, of course, when he can… Families, I'm sure, will want to… There have been certain, that is, different… There will be certain *changes* for Juan Miguel to adjust to…" The confused thought that this, too, was part of the prank had a painfully short life span and lay dead already; even if Buht had tried to entertain that hope, the creeping terrible tightness at his throat would have made it impossible.

"They say his parents were out of town," a colleague leaned up to say, as they filed like shades out of the gym. Buht walked ahead quickly, acknowledging no one, and the colleague fell back in step with another teacher.

"…in Namibia on safari…" Buht heard. "…no one to call…"

"…found bloody by the highway to Cuernavaca." The teacher had dropped his voice, but it was as if Buht had speakers hooked up to it. "Two fingers missing, not to mention…"

"Oh God … intercept *that* package…"

Everywhere, children were weeping, adults who looked suddenly like children. Teachers were wrapped together, on pathways, in doorways; Brazil was puking into the bougainvillea, dropped onto his knees, Coach Araya's hand on his back. Elaine the librarian was wailing like a biblical woman at the top of the upper-school stairs, her arms flung out. People crowded around and Buht was pulled up with the tide of them. At one point her hot, wet eye socket found his shoulder bone, but he ducked out from under. "No, no, shh, you had to turn him in that time, he understood," the reading tutor soothed, in answer to the librarian's regretful rant. One of Buht's freshman, the runty German exchange student, streaming from the mouth and nose, spotted him and ran at Buht, who resisted a bullfighter dodge; the kid wrapped onto him like a starfish, snotting his shirtfront. Buht laid a quavering hand on his head.

Buht wouldn't wait for the mail to come. He didn't wait for the final bell. He left by the bus entrance and hopped a cab home and walked and shat his dogs and rebuilt the boxes he'd collapsed in the laundry room and had his shit packed and neatly in his truck by nine P.M. He'd always been good spatially. I'll leave in the morning, he resolved, but by quarter to eleven that night he was paying the Cuautitlán toll. But why the hell would he call me? Buht asked himself, again and again and again on the drive north, his throat aching, vision blurring, no less any of the times. Needless to say, he did not stop off in the old mining town Real de Catorce as the burned-out ceramics teacher had coached, did not bunk in with a one-eyed philosopher named Giuseppe at the end of the town's last lane, didn't count to the forty-ninth lamppost on the approach to Tanque de Dolores, where dusty peyote plants should be thick at the base of each gobernadora plant. *Me, why me?* Rather, Buht did about eight hundred miles a day, at eighty, eyes straight ahead, working to police his treacherous imagination. *His uncle?* Often, he drove in silence. Paul Simon's "America," which he'd had scheduled for when he neared the border, sounded like a nursery rhyme. Heroica Guaymas. Sonoyta, Sonora. There were eleven missed calls from Chloe Turner before he turned his phone off. Within a hundred miles of the border, checkpoints were thicker; crocodile-looking soldiers with helmets nearly met by their wool dust masks, just their eyes peeping over, now and then poked at his duffels with the barrels of their rifles, as Chops and Flow went mad. All he could do, absurdly, drawing little comfort, surely lost in translation, was swear to all and any that he would never set foot in Mexico again, that it had been an error, a blip—Officer, I swear to try never even to think of it. Hermosillo, Baja California. *But why in hell would he say I was his uncle?* asked Buht of himself as the border came into view. *Why in hell, in hell?* He was openly weeping. *Uncle? Uncle!* He found the bandanna he used to clean his Oakleys, pressed it to his eyes, merged left into the lane for those with nothing to declare.

Tony Hoagland

WHITE WRITER

Obviously, it's a category I've been made aware of
                                        from time to time.

It's been pointed out that my characters eat a lot of lightly braised asparagus

and get FedEx packages almost daily.

Yet I *dislike* being thought of as a white writer.

Has it made it easier for me to publish?
                                        Oh, probably so.
But I get tired of publishing in White-
                        Only magazines.

When I find my books in the White Literature section of the bookstore,
                                        how do I feel?
I thought I was writing about more than that.

Tax refunds, Spanish lessons, premature ejaculation;

I know some readers need to see their lives reflected on the page—
                meat loaf and sitcoms; the fear of perishing.

It lets them know they aren't alone.

The art it takes to make that kind of comfort
                        is not something I look upon with scorn.

But after a while, you start to feel like white
                        is all you'll ever be in the world.

And gradually,
after all the struggling against
                  the dread of being what you are

you accept it, it becomes you.

Then, with fresh determination, you lean forward again.

You write whiter and whiter.

WILLA

WILLA

WILLA

I LOVE

WILLA

FROM THE ARCHIVE
OF WILLA KIM

curated by

Nicole Rudick

———

A native of Los Angeles, Willa Kim made her first trip to Europe in 1952, at the age of thirty-five. She traveled with a friend, the painter Margaret Stark. Paris was their first destination. "All the artists we admired were in Paris," she recalls. "And everything French was worshipped on the West Coast." Near the end of her trip, she was invited to a Thanksgiving dinner by the expatriate fashion illustrator Tom Keogh and his wife, Theodora. It was there she met William Pène du Bois, the first art director of the newly launched *Paris Review*, to which Tom had contributed several drawings of Paris life.

In truth, Willa had already been introduced to Pène du Bois, briefly: he had helped give her and Margaret a send-off when they made a trip to Spain. But that Thanksgiving, she says, was when she really met him. Billy showed her Paris and took her to a party celebrating the inaugural issue of the magazine. Of the first issue, Willa recalls, "Billy said all they [the editors] were doing was arguing with each other and they could never get anything published. He said that he finally got so sick of it that he just decided to have it printed—and he did! When he showed it at their next gathering, they were stunned. There it was—*The Paris Review.*"

Willa soon returned to New York, followed by Pène du Bois. They were married in 1955. Billy's uncle Raoul Pène du Bois, a legendary art director and costumer, helped Willa gain a foothold in the world of New York theater and ballet. Over a half century—during which she made costumes for Glen Tetley, Mary Alice, Jack Lemmon, Birgit Keil, Evelyn Cisneros, and others—she garnered Tonys, Emmys, and an Obie, and was inducted into the Theater Hall of Fame in 2007.

Together, Willa and Billy maintained a trove of work from the early years of the *Review* and from their respective artistic careers. What follows here is a motley selection of art, photographs, and ephemera from their collection.

Paris scene by Tom Keogh.

Above: Costume rendering by Willa Kim for *Under the Sun* (1976),
a ballet tribute to Alexander Calder's sculptures and mobiles.

The costumes consisted of white leotards individually hand painted by Kim, a process
she pioneered with this show. "We first did all the fittings on the dancer, marking the
patterns on them, because you take a unitard or a pair of tights, and you don't know where
the knee is, you don't know where the thighs are, you don't know where the musculature is.
Then I had the costume shop bring in mannequins and we put the tights and things on
and painted in the colors. It was quite a revolution for choreographers to see this. They realized
that there was something up there that they hadn't seen before."

Right: Plimpton as a premier danseur. Collage by William Pène du Bois and Richard Marshall,
who served as the *Review*'s art editor from 1978 to 1993.

MY GOD, IT'S PLIMPTON!

William Pène du Bois

Above: A lithograph for William Pène du Bois and his first wife, Jane, by Tom Keogh in 1952.

Left: *Paris Review* tattoo, courtesy William Pène du Bois and Richard Marshall.

Above and following spread: Costume renderings by Willa Kim
for *The Old Glory* (1964), a play by Robert Lowell.
Right: Unidentified caricature by William Pène du Bois.

Dear Jonathan.

I've done tons of research on American Indians, particularly with East coast indians – They were almost naked – a few feathers & fringes – a blanket draped around – Tatoos – ~~??~~ a lot of the research is misleading – but amusing – Europeans ideas of what indians wore – I think we can do anything you want. These may be too silly. any way see you next week.

Della.

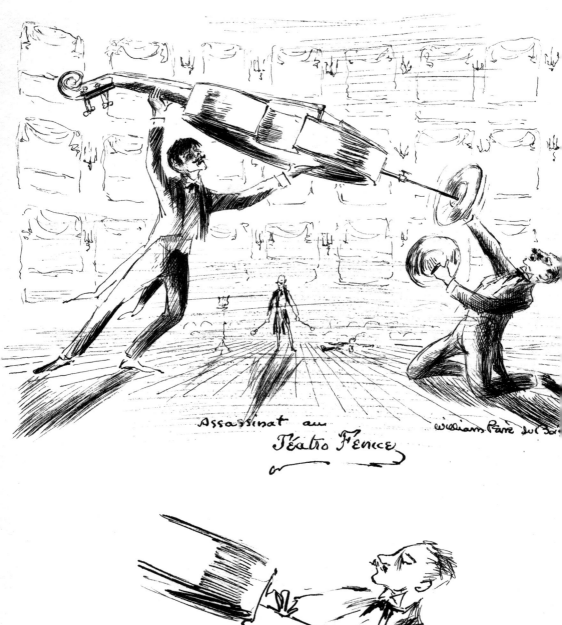

Assassinat au
Téatro Fenice

Above: Album cover (notional?) by Tom Keogh.

Left: Assassinat au Téatro Fenice by William Pène du Bois.

MY GOD, IT'S PLIMPTON!

Above: Plimpton and James Cagney. Collage by William Pène du Bois and Richard Marshall.
Right: Paris scene by Tom Keogh.

Above: Paris scene by Tom Keogh.

Right: *Paris Review* tattoo, courtesy William Pène du Bois and Richard Marshall.

William Pène du Bois

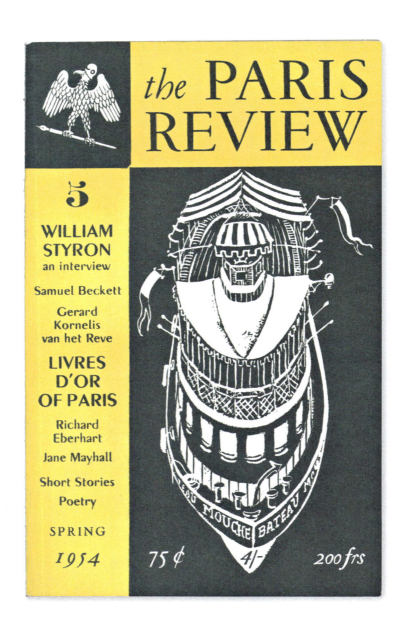

The cover of issue 5 reads:

the PARIS REVIEW

5

WILLIAM STYRON
an interview

Samuel Beckett

Gerard
Kornelis
van het Reve

**LIVRES
D'OR
OF PARIS**

Richard
Eberhart

Jane Mayhall

Short Stories

Poetry

SPRING
1954

75 ¢   4/-   200 frs

William Pène du Bois's painting of a *bateau mouche* (*right*)
for the cover of issue 5.

75 ¢   4/-   200 frs

Frederick Seidel

PUSSY DAYS

Putting my lenses in, I see No Man's Land in the mirror—
Which makes me think of times in Tokyo so long ago
When, on some subway station platform, in a crowd,
Not finding a single person who spoke English
To ask how I could get to somewhere,
For a panicked several minutes
I experienced near-weightlessness and something quite like bliss.

Once, in India, I crossed a midday plaza—
This was Mumbai, then still called Bombay—
And there were maybe 25,000 people, myself the only white,
And no one in the mob of brown giving me a thought.
I walked invisibly through the Indian indifference.
I crossed across the packed brown Bombay busyness—
A man who wanted to be No Man's Land, free at last.

Now listen, do the right thing, you're a gentleman, be a gentleman.
Empty yourself of meaning
And be a man without ideas.
I went from Bali to Bombay, already sick with something,
From Bombay to Cairo, getting sicker.
Next, on to Tehran, where rooms constantly tilted.
Ah, Shireen, one-night stand of the Shah, looking as if

She had just stepped out of a swimming pool always.
Many swallow-tailed footmen served much caviar.
Among us in the tent was a spy of the Shah.
I was murmuring hurrah,
Once I learned the guest pretending to be drunk was a spy of the Shah.
Then came the revolution
And Reza Pahlavi fled, and rather soon after came cancer.

And then, poor Shah, came cancer—and looking for an answer.
My doctor in New York was summoned to Mexico City with others
From around the world, but they were not permitted to examine the Shah,
But they could ask him how he was feeling.
Doctors from around the world
Were not allowed to see the Shah undressed
And see the nothingness.

My celebrity GP treated heads of state and me.
One patient was Fiat's Gianni Agnelli, who gave the doctor a Ferrari.
Nothing was the matter with me,
But something is the matter with me.
The Shah needed a splenectomy.
One would eventually be performed in Egypt but too late,
A spleen removal done by a cardiac surgeon, Michael DeBakey the Great.

I, too, took a sickness with me for three years around the world,
But the tropical diseases man at New York Hospital,
After months of tests, couldn't find anything the matter.
It doesn't matter.
I was looking at No Man's Land
Between the trenches and World War I will never end.
Millions are already dead. Hemingway is writing instead.

The tropical diseases man who found nothing the matter
Became the second doctor of mine summoned south of the border.
Tropical-Disease-Man, by proposing
That the United States, on humanitarian grounds, let the murderer
And torturer into the country for treatment—which then happened—
Helped incite the calamitous Islamist
Takeover of the U.S. embassy.

I long for Hemingway in Paris.
I long for Paris and everywhere else that no longer matters.
I long for the stupid English and the French
And the trenches and the stench.
I long for *A Farewell to Arms* and the sadness as simple as a rainbow,
And rowing across the lake at night with Catherine Barkley, who will die.
My fellow Americans, cry with me for pussy days gone by.

Women sunbathe along the shore of a deep blue sea.
The eyelid of the day blinks on the blue to signify another tropical day.
A mind green as a golf course bakes in the hot sun and from the green
Rises a perfume of luscious and obscene
Pages turning and the woman's legs open and the reader reads the poem.
Something is the matter with me.
I'm too happy.

Pound and Hemingway and Joyce in Paris lassoed
And branded the goddamned English language—cowboys in *Paree!*
Each fellow had his favorite café where he liked to be.
At the top of the stairs leading up to the street from the metro,
French riot police, squatting behind a machine gun on a tripod,
Waiting no doubt for some Algerian, swiveled the gun around to aim at me
On a lovely summer's day in 1960.

I immediately looked behind me to show them you boys don't want me!
I was being stabbed in the stomach, the room was spinning,
And, according to the tests, nothing was the matter.
Tropical-Disease-Man joked: "Maybe you got bitten by a shark in Bali!"
Twenty little schoolchildren in Connecticut were slaughtered last Friday.
Things happen even in Bali
When you write poetry.

Maybe the world got bitten by a shark.
I'm taking off from Newark Liberty International Airport.
The captain has turned the seat belt sign off while we're still climbing.
I'm opening the emergency-exit door located nearest me
To wing-walk above the Statue of Liberty
And the bountiful chemical factories of New Jersey.
I've reached the altitude of No Man's Land and I'm seeking asylum.

Bards response in reverse (with name kept boldface):

Kcab cipe nikcuf ruo tnaw ew – **OXOX**!

- Ike's exhorting the bards
- Ike's hortatory apostrophe to the bards
- The echolalic call-and-response between Ike and the bards
- Ike – [doomed] pensive, introverted, diffident, reticent Taurus; coy fanatic; implacable [neo-pagan] [polytheist], obsessive, solipsistic, out of touch with the world, relentlessly and tediously indecipherable… blathering opacity…
- Profane language? (4)
- [To give vent to] [A full-bore venting] to all his febrile antipathies… celebrities are disgusting and decadent. And his (and La Felina's) zealous anti-elitism.
- Bard recapitulate Ike who recapitulates the bards.
- XOXO's ventriloquism
- the echolalic call-and-response chants to the mesmerizing beat of empty can against spokes, etc.
- Every unknown plebian is a hero by virtue of his or her anonymity

Ike, here, is essentially pulling himself out of his own ass – in such a way that he's inside-out. The mobius strip, the hero/bard, etc. "The fact that the bards are represented here as repeating what Ike says but

The Art of Fiction No. 219

———

MARK LEYNER

Mark Leyner's name has been familiar to readers of experimental fiction since 1995, when he published his first story collection, *I Smell Esther Williams*, but it was his second collection, *My Cousin, My Gastroenterologist* (with its memorable opening riff: "I was an infinitely hot and dense dot" raised by "huge and lurid puppets"), followed by the novel *Et Tu, Babe*, that made him one of the most acclaimed and publicized writers of that decade. Profiled in major magazines, Leyner also appeared on late-night talk shows and in a contentious segment of *Charlie Rose* alongside David Foster Wallace and Jonathan Franzen.

After a second novel, *The Tetherballs of Bougainville*, was published in 1998, Leyner dropped away from the literary world. He worked in Hollywood, where one of his cowritten scripts, *War, Inc.*, was made into a movie starring John Cusack. Leyner also coauthored a series of best-selling medical humor books beginning with *Why Do Men Have Nipples? Hundreds of Questions You'd Only Ask a Doctor After Your Third Martini*.

Fourteen years after *Tetherballs*, Leyner returned with *The Sugar Frosted Nutsack*, both an epic and the exegesis of an epic. It begins when a claque of gods (with names like Fast-Cooking Ali and XOXO) return from "spring break" to create a universe whose mortal hero is an unemployed butcher in Jersey City. Reviewing *The Sugar Frosted Nutsack* in the *New York Times Book Review*, Ben Marcus wrote that Leyner "demonstrates how much is still possible for the novel when tradition is left behind, proving that fiction can be robust, provocative and staggeringly inventive, without for a moment forfeiting entertainment."

The bulk of this interview took place at the Elysian Cafe, a bistro across the street from Leyner's home in Hoboken, New Jersey. Born in 1956, Leyner, a self-described "gym rat," is handsome, smallish, and very fit, with muscular arms that in many lifting circles would qualify as "guns." He seemed both proud and sheepish about them, the type of contradiction that, as the conversation developed, Leyner revealed as a central tension in his life and his writing.

—*Sam Lipsyte*

LEYNER

Let me tell you about my morning.

INTERVIEWER

Let me ask. How was your morning?

LEYNER

Funny you ask. I had a meeting this morning with my editor, Michael Pietsch. I really like having a breakfast meeting. First of all, it's caffeine and not alcohol. It's more what a businessman would do. Otherwise, I just basically wander around in my pajamas.

INTERVIEWER

So you've been to Manhattan and back today, back for your lunch meeting.

Yeah. I'm just a dynamo. I've done fifty critically important things already today, including this terrific meeting this morning about what my next book should be. I've just decided—and this is a huge scoop for *The Paris Review*, because Michael Pietsch and I just made this decision—I've just decided that I'm going to write a book about Mussolini.

INTERVIEWER

About Mussolini.

LEYNER

Yeah. The web of my own life and the web of his life.

INTERVIEWER

Why Mussolini? Have you been thinking about him since you were a kid?

LEYNER

No, that would be too weird. Mom, read me that manifesto. Dad, put on the black shirt again. Sing me that song. But I'm fascinated by demagogues. I've seen some of Fidel's speeches where he'd harangue crowds of people in the blazing Havana sun for seven hours. He'd speak extemporaneously about very technical agricultural issues for hours.

INTERVIEWER

I think of that footage of Mussolini skiing shirtless in the Alps.

LEYNER

You know who has a similar theatrics of masculinity is Putin. He's always shirtless, hunting in Siberia shirtless or something—Boy, I'm hot!

INTERVIEWER

So this book will be about masculinity, or models of masculinity?

LEYNER

Something like that. I think I have a particular interest in dictators— generally, in worlds of violence and physical prowess, because that's all so much what I feel I'm not. Then again, there were enormous shelves of books in the houses of my parents and my grandparents, and that, too, seemed completely unattainable, such an exotic, unattainable endeavor, writing a book. Almost everything I do can be analyzed on this grid, as a response to this ambivalence about the sort of man I'm supposed to be. I'll die with this not reconciled.

INTERVIEWER

You were made to feel not tough enough?

LEYNER

I think I was, for perfectly good reasons. I was a small, sensitive kid close to his mom. This is all textbook, the first child in the extended family, *le petit prince*.

INTERVIEWER

Sorry, this Richie Sambora solo is getting to me.

LEYNER

Should I ask her to turn it down a little? She could. Wait, here she comes. [*To waitress*] Can you do me a tiny favor?

WAITRESS

Sure.

LEYNER

We're doing this interview. Do you think you could turn that down a *tiny* bit?

WAITRESS

Yeah.

INTERVIEWER

Do you always have one project in mind? Or a steady stream of possibilities?

LEYNER

The steady stream doesn't work for me. I do write all the time. Some of it is connected thematically to what I did the day before—often not. It's just what I always have, an accumulation of material to rummage through.

So there are troves of it.

There's one trove. Some artists—Cornell, Rauschenberg—used to find things in the street or in flea markets, some kind of cultural detritus to bring back and look at and juxtapose with other things. I do something similar.

Leyner, age eleven. "Growing up in houses where, at dinner, people are asked, Do you have any good stories? And people trade elaborate jokes back and forth. That's the world I come from."

But I have to make my own garbage to sift through. Things I overhear, things I've overheard that I've misremembered.

But you used a good word that I responded to. I said, "That doesn't work for me." What was that?

A stream? A steady stream?

LEYNER

A forceful stream, I think they say in urology. In response to what you were saying about the forceful, steady stream, I think there has to be some kind of crisis before I really feel there's a book I should write. When I started, I wanted to see if a certain kind of line, shaded with poetry, could sustain itself in prose. Not out of idle curiosity—I thought it would be a wonderful thing. The poetry I read and the music I listened to had an immersive, unmodulated intensity to them, and I wanted to do that in prose. After several books, I felt that I had explored this notion.

INTERVIEWER

Had you proven to yourself you could do it?

LEYNER

At a certain point after I wrote *The Tetherballs of Bougainville*, I wasn't feeling the urgency anymore. That had something to do with why I stopped. I had been doing a little movie stuff, a lot of magazine work. In fact there was a whole collection of magazine work, *Tooth Imprints on a Corn Dog*. I think out of everything I've done, that book gives me qualms. I don't know why.

INTERVIEWER

Can you speculate?

LEYNER

Because it exists under the sign of an American magazine culture.

INTERVIEWER

I've always wondered about your magazine writing. I understand why every magazine wanted you, but I wondered if you felt constrained by your assignments.

LEYNER

I had to think of myself as an architect who had a client and the client had certain requirements, but they had hired me because there was something unique about my work and they wanted that inflection. So whether that's "Shouts & Murmurs" or back pages for *Time*, that's what I did. I don't know if this is true for every writer, but my writing and the way I configure myself, my pride in myself and my identity—those things are very interwoven.

At some point I didn't like being some go-to funny magazine guy. It didn't comport with how I felt as an artist, as a writer. But I wasn't bad at it. I'm a good guy, first of all. I'm sort of responsible. If someone needed a "Shouts & Murmurs" or a *Time* magazine back page or something for *Esquire*, I wouldn't just send them a bunch of my stuff and say, Put that on the back page or don't bother me. I'd try to do it for them. Using that architect analogy, if a woman comes and says, My husband is nonambulatory, so we need ramps in the house and things like that, you have to say, Okay. You can't be—well, you *could* be sadistic and perverse and make a house that's even harder to navigate, but...

INTERVIEWER

To stretch that metaphor, a lot of architects make work that fits the specifications of the client, and then they also design, perhaps, buildings that might never be built. But your fiction gets to be published and shown so it's not quite the same. Or is it?

LEYNER

I was always completely divided and somewhat confounded by the fact that I was getting opportunities to write for these magazines or to go on television based on this work of mine. I thought that was the most amazing thing. Now I think it was really kind of aberrant. That doesn't usually happen to writers who are adventurous in a formal way, who aren't just straight-up realistic, denotative writers.

INTERVIEWER

I don't think anybody's going on television anymore.

LEYNER

No, no one is. And it used to be fairly common. If you wrote a novel, at the very least you could be on the *Today* show for five, ten minutes.

You made the rounds.

It was an enormous rush to be asked to do all of these things. And it was happening in this fast and furious way. It took me a while to sit back and think about it.

It all shows up in transformed ways in your books. *Tetherballs* took those forms you were working in—magazines, scripts—and worked them brilliantly from a fictional standpoint.

That's much better said than I could ever say it. You don't even need me for this.

I would add that some of the first commercial work I did had nothing to do with magazines at all—it was advertising.

Do you see a similarity between poetry and advertising? In both cases you're working in a limited amount of space and trying to get the most bang for your buck, in a sense, from language.

That's an idealized version of advertising. I like *Mad Men* as much as the next guy, but when Don Draper sits back smugly and delivers what's supposed to be a devastatingly brilliant campaign and insights into consumer psychology, I'm not that impressed by it. I think what I liked best about those years was maneuvering through office politics. It gave me an opportunity to act out—and get out of my system—this notion of what a man does. As I started to say before, I grew up with a very clear, almost Lévi-Straussian idea that there were two kinds of men, two archetypes, a paired opposition. And I think I've tried in some way or another to be both.

You know this word *luftmensch*?

A dreamer?

A dreamer, a kind of intellectual, someone who just sits at home and reads the Yiddish papers and for whom any kind of practical endeavor is impossible. Fixing anything in the house—impossible. Making any kind of money—impossible. Which was very appealing. It seemed like a beautiful life to me. Then on the other hand, and completely polar to that, was the *shtarker*, tougher, a sort of businessperson who had a strange, murky, unidentifiable business. If you look at a book like *My Cousin*, it's got all the aggressiveness and impertinence of the quasi–mob guy sitting on his stoop at the end of the day in a wifebeater and the lyrical musings of the luftmensch model, mashed up together.

Not just in *Cousin*.

In everything I do. And I think in *The Sugar Frosted Nutsack* I actually made a character who represents, who embodies, both those things for the first time.

Then the gods are kind of tough guys. And the drug-addled bards are maybe more luftmenschen?

It's a big, ongoing problem for me. I think being short led me toward the question of how I could be tough, how I could have a forceful kind of physicality. And yet that's all very alien to my predilections, which are just to keep to myself and be a sweet, sensitive Proustian boy with his mom. Trailing along behind his mom at Saks Fifth Avenue, tugging at her skirts, asking, Can we go home now?

Did your parents grow up here?

My parents did, and their parents did not. And men like my father—young, ambitious, virile men—were aspiring to the white-collar *nomenklatura*, which would have been unheard-of in previous generations. Also, my father had been a musician earlier in his life, and my mother had wanted to be an artist, so I was aware of Pollock and de Kooning and certain kinds of jazz. My parents seemed to me like Rob and Laura Petrie. When I watch *The Dick Van Dyke Show*, it seemed like it was about them. They were dashing figures to me—not glamorous in terms of being wealthy, but hip, youthful, intellectually and culturally inquisitive people.

INTERVIEWER

They were young?

LEYNER

They were young for parents. When I was in high school, they were in their thirties. Everyone would come over and say, Oh, you have such cool parents. I had the least tortured upbringing I can imagine. It was really sort of paradise for me.

[*A man familiar to Leyner enters the Elysian Cafe. Leyner hails him from our table, nodding toward his bandaged wrist.*]

LEYNER

Hey, dude, what happened? What's on your wrist?

MAN

I just dropped a…

LEYNER

This is Sam Lipsyte. We're doing an interview, a conversation. You want to say something?

MAN

I have a herpetic lesion on my—

LEYNER

Show us. Sam's an amateur dermatological proctologist. He specializes in lesions on the buttocks.

INTERVIEWER

In fact, I just started today, so...

MAN

Excellent!

INTERVIEWER

So, if you don't mind I could—

LEYNER

Can you warm up a knife so it's blazing hot and we'll take a look?

MAN

Notice how you put yourself in, too. "We'll take a look." *You're* not a proctologist.

LEYNER

No, but he needs an assistant.

MAN

Anyway, we listened to you on the way home yesterday, on audiobook.

LEYNER

Oh, you bought that? Is it any good?

MAN

It's really good.

LEYNER

[*To interviewer*] Have you recorded your books?

INTERVIEWER

Yes, my last one.

LEYNER

It's such a grueling thing to do, right? Because it's not a real audience. The right way to do it, I think, would be with a live audience.

INTERVIEWER

Like Castro.

LEYNER

Exactly. You have to force them to stay.

MAN

They did *Great Gatsby*.

LEYNER

In its entirety?

MAN

Yes. They read it and acted it at the same time. It was fantastic.

LEYNER

Who did? Various celebrities?

MAN

Uh, yeah.

LEYNER

The Kardashians?

INTERVIEWER

They're still doing it.

LEYNER

They're still doing it meaning they still haven't finished … as we speak?

MAN

[*To interviewer*] Nice to meet you.

LEYNER

Talk to you later. Where were we?

[*Distracted, Leyner points to a man in a postal uniform who is taking a stool at the bar.*] Hey, there's my mailman, right there! He's going to sit down, have some drinks. That's why we never get our mail!

INTERVIEWER

It'll get there eventually.

LEYNER

No one uses mail anymore anyway.

INTERVIEWER

I remember first coming across your work in the late eighties, in *Fiction International*.

LEYNER

There was a time when I thought that if I could have anything in *Fiction International*, I'd be happy. I'd make a pact with God. It seemed like one of these unattainable things, to be in there with Raymond Federman or Russell Edson—remember how he wrote those gnomic little paragraphs?—and Gilbert Sorrentino, Ronald Sukenick. Those guys.

INTERVIEWER

That's a whole world. Or a few worlds.

LEYNER

I thought, Ah, wouldn't it be nice someday to get a nod from these guys?

INTERVIEWER

There are many moments like that when you're young and starting out.

LEYNER

When I started this book, *The Sugar Frosted Nutsack*, I was feeling very much back in that time. I had no idea what interest there would be in a book of mine, or if there'd be some hostility to me, or if I could even do this.

Was that invigorating?

It was fantastic. This last book is a very pure, very true example of my work at its most forceful. And what the work also means to me as a person. I backed myself into this corner, from which I then felt comfortable fighting myself out. Did I tell you this story about the giant cockroach in Jamaica?

I don't think so.

When I was at Brandeis, I met this girl named Rachel Horowitz, and we really loved reggae music. This was in 1970. We decided, Why don't we go to Jamaica? So we went and we got some really nifty little bungalow place in Montego Bay—very cheap, because we couldn't afford much then. And it had a little pool for the couple of bungalows and a little kitchen. And I'd never really stayed in place like this on my own, with a girlfriend. I mean, nothing quite like that. I had been away the year before with another girl, took a trip to Israel and in Europe and things, but I'd never been in a groovy tropical place like this. And we had a car, so one day we drove into town and got some stuff, because we had a refrigerator and a pantry. We also got some Red Stripe. And this guy at Brandeis had given me some acid to bring to Jamaica. This guy was the Johnny Appleseed of acid. He wanted everyone to take acid. He was always giving acid to people. He would take a load of acid and explain an album cover to you for just *hours*. He would take a Hot Tuna album that you had seen a trillion times and he would begin to examine it with these long lectures that were like Fidel Castro giving a lecture at the Sorbonne. He also once set his hand on fire and watched it for quite a while because he was so high. That really impressed me. Anyway, this guy had given me some acid and one night, when Rachel and I were just hanging out, I said, You wanna take some? She said no. I said, Okay, I think I'm going to. So I took it, and it comes on, and then I want a beer and I go into the little kitchen, and by now the acid's *full* on and this bug, this big flying cockroach, like a palmetto bug—you know those things?—it crawls out of the six-pack, and to me, at the time, it was like a pterodactyl, like in some Raquel Welch movie set in prehistoric times. According to Rachel, I battled this thing in the little kitchen for, like, five hours. She heard pans and things breaking and she said I emerged with a torn shirt, sweaty—and victorious. That's what my experience of writing *The Sugar Frosted Nutsack* was like. Battling this pterodactyl in the closet with a pan. At a certain point, of course, the book attained a mind of its own, a subjectivity or an autocatalytic, machinelike quality.

INTERVIEWER

Then you just have to feed it.

LEYNER

Yeah, but don't get your arm caught! Because it'll take it right off.

INTERVIEWER

It'll eat anything.

LEYNER

As I was saying, before the book was really underway, it felt like being back in the day, like being young. Me against the world. Because when I started the book I was at wit's end. My back was against the wall. I needed to use my purest and most deadly kung fu.

INTERVIEWER

Your secret style. It seems like you experienced a different literary culture back when your earlier books were coming out.

LEYNER

When *My Cousin* and *Et Tu, Babe* came out, I was on *Letterman*. I read from one of my books on *Conan*. I almost lost my place, thinking, How fucking great is this? You're reading from one of your books on television. But I would also think, Why did I ever even want this? I'd just rather be home. We wouldn't do what we do if we loved being with people. We like to be by ourselves.

I've always said I became a writer so that I wouldn't have to speak to people in person.

Exactly. But you teach now.

I teach, yes. Did you ever do any teaching?

At a signing in New York in 1993.

Very little. I did it in graduate school because I had a teaching fellowship. When I first moved to Hoboken, I was an adjunct at Brooklyn College. Students love me the first time around, because I'm entertaining, but then they get wise to me. I don't really have any interest in reading their stuff. I did this thing for a while in Toronto, where they put us up in a really nice hotel and paid for everything, and then paid us a bunch of money. I would just have students read what they wrote, out loud in class, which I thought was brilliant because then I didn't have to actually read it in the hotel. People seem okay with that kind of thing for a while. But ultimately they turn on me.

INTERVIEWER

Complaints?

LEYNER

They turn on me. I have to leave town in the middle of the night, or they'll string me up by my feet like Mussolini.

INTERVIEWER

Tie you up with your mistress.

LEYNER

Exactly. I have multilevel affinities with Mussolini, actually—fear of being run out of town with my mistress and being strung up by my feet.

INTERVIEWER

Recently I saw the movie *War, Inc.*, which you cowrote. In the first few minutes John Cusack says he feels like a "character from a Céline novel." Was that your line?

LEYNER

That's something Cusack might have improvised. I think Cusack and I had a conversation once about Céline. It always surprises people that some artist they like is a Fascist. It's always unpleasant news you have to deliver to somebody. And I think I had to tell him.

"Sorry, man."

"I think you should sit down." But wait—doesn't that line also mention *The Island of Dr. Moreau*? It does. I remember. I think that must be me. If not, it's a Leyner plagiarist.

There were a lot of projects that never got made, right?

There was this one thing, about a guy sort of based on John Lydon, Johnny Rotten, only he was a virtuoso surgeon who did his surgeries in an actual theater, transposing the idea of a medical theater into a real theater. It was called *Iggy Vile M.D.* That was the first script I wrote. MTV bought it and made a pilot, then it sort of died. Although one of the executives at MTV said it was the most revolting thing he'd ever seen.

Do you have a copy?

Yeah. And actually, it's not that revolting. It was just prescient in its revoltingness. It had a great scene, which I'm still proud of. There's a club or restaurant that Iggy Vile would go to, and at the club there's a ring, and two martial arts guys fight, and then the loser is slaughtered and served. That's the fare of the restaurant. And that's where Iggy Vile would go. He's there with a friend, drinking and talking, and a woman, a fat woman, comes up and says, "You're Iggy Vile, the great surgeon! Iggy Vile, M.D." And he says, "Fuck off, I'm drinking with my mate here." And she comes back and says, "Oh please, please, Iggy, I've spent my whole adult life trying to slim down in every possible way. I've done the grapefruit diet and the Beverly Hills Diet, and I've had the gastric surgery and staples and nothing's worked. You're the last hope for me." And she bothers him until finally he turns her around and bends her over, and he takes a straw from his friend's drink, and he jabs it into her ass, and he sucks the fat out of her, and he spits it into a pitcher in the middle of the table. And we made the stuff! We made the stuff that looked like fat! It's pretty wonderful to watch. That's the scene I admire. I take a certain amount of childlike sadistic pleasure in thinking I've caused all of these people to spend their time and money making a thing like that. It's like de Sade in prison getting all the other inmates to perform his plays.

INTERVIEWER

That might be the real seduction in film and television. But I wanted to ask you about literary influences.

LEYNER

I used to have this little pen. It was a Yankees pen—I was a Yankees fanatic as a little boy—and I had a game I would play endlessly in my room. My right hand was the pitcher—I used it to flick a marble—and my left hand was the batter. And I would announce the whole game. Three batters an inning, both sides, it could take two hours. And I'd do this little thing at the beginning of the game where I'd talk about injuries and what to expect and how people are feeling. I'd do the whole thing myself, for my own delectation. I think these are the things that are the precursors to writing. People ask, What writers inspired you? But it happens deeper and earlier than that. The important things antecede reading. Growing up in houses where, at dinner, people are asked, Do you have any good stories? And people trade elaborate jokes back and forth. That's the world I come from.

For a while, I would decapitate my sister's dolls. That was a little French Revolution period. I'm still in that period.

INTERVIEWER

So you don't have any influences?

LEYNER

I have some. What was that stuff that Dennis Hopper would inhale in *Blue Velvet*? Amyl nitrite? If I need something like the literary equivalent of poppers it tends to be Wallace Stevens. I started with poetry—a concentrated, brilliantly titrated dose of very compressed language.

What were you writing before *I Smell Esther Williams*—straight narrative stuff, or poetry?

LEYNER

I wrote poems. I don't think I could recover from the embarrassment of reading those. And then I wrote a column for my high-school paper that was a half-fictionalized, half-journalistic, fragmented account of what my friends and I would do. I had an interest then—I still do, you can see it in almost everything I've written—in what happens if you use certain forms from public discourse in the world of intimacy, or intimate discourse in public. When I was in junior high school, I would read these big interviews in *Rolling Stone*. They would always be called "The Pete Townshend Interview" or "The Keith Richards Interview." I used to think, What if you just picked someone, some kid in high school, and did a massive interview with him, just about things in his life? Today, because of reality TV, that doesn't seem so mind-boggling. But it was an interesting idea then, and one that I've played with. *Et Tu, Babe* is really just an involuted elaboration of that idea.

INTERVIEWER

The Sugar Frosted Nutsack strikes me as different from your earlier books. While it certainly partakes of pop-cultural allusions and the like, it doesn't play as fast and loose with them as earlier works do. It seems more interested in accruing its own distinct set of resonances with the constant recursion of its storytelling. It's not that you are avoiding naming the things and the brands of the world, so much as you don't seem as concerned about precisely which associations we can all agree on.

LEYNER

When I started writing this book, I realized that, for the first time, I was going to have to forget the notion of a consensual canon of imagery and allusion and citations. Instead, I was going to just write the book using what I use and not worry about it.

What happened in the culture in those fourteen years between *Tetherballs* and *Nutsack*?

A couple of things. When I first started publishing my work, I had a very definite feeling of surfing the zeitgeist, of being fluent in all the prevailing memes. This might have been completely delusory, but it's how I felt—that I was, in some very essential way, plugged into the culture. And it also seemed to me a time when people my age, people "in my grade," as we used to say, had ascended to significant positions at magazines and publishing houses. So I felt as if there were a very specific and kindred and somewhat influential audience out there for me. And this audience and I were very much in sync. These were people who'd watched the same TV shows as I did as a kid, read the same comics, listened to the same music. There were all of these shared allusions and references I felt I could count on. But this audience has become more diffuse as we all age, and various strata of younger people enter into the mix. More to the point, the culture has become balkanized, so there's no possibility of surfing *the* zeitgeist because there is no one zeitgeist, there's a plurality of zeitgeists. There's no real question now of cultural fluency—that notion seems completely quaint and archaic today. So my feelings about writing from some privileged cultural perspective for an identifiable, kindred, and optimally receptive audience have changed completely. Now I feel like a completely alienated and marginalized person who traffics in some form of discredited esoterica. But I'm much happier!

There's another issue people sometimes bring up with me, which is the ascendance of the Internet and how somehow I was prescient about the phenomenon of Google, hypertext, and so on. The idea being that the kinds of radical tangentiality and manic eclecticism that you could say characterize my "style" are now available to anyone who goes online, that anyone can now cobble together a lyrical sentence comprising references to Jivaro tribesmen, stigmata, male lactation, Julius Evola, the hair-plucking ceremonies of Jain nuns, *Don Kirshner's Rock Concert*, or what have you. I have my doubts about all this. I've always been after a methodology that was about evading my own taste and escaping from my own predilections and cultivating mutations and maximizing accidents. The search engine, it seems to me, is all about goal-orientated efficiency, rote procedures, and the reinforcement of habit. I would much rather depend on the serendipity offered by the chance physical proximity of disparate volumes in an old library, of basically lurching in the dark. It's all about getting lost for me. Efficacy is the mortal enemy of my style.

INTERVIEWER

So you don't think the world's become Leynerized?

LEYNER

We're living in a world in which we're all surveilled, targeted, herded, and indoctrinated to an unprecedented degree. Our fallen, debased state is ghastly. Our bodies have been transformed into profit-optimized enterprise zones, our minds have been hacked and neutered, our social milieus have been completely leached of authenticity. Leynerized? I fucking hope not.

INTERVIEWER

I take it you're not delighted with the state of things.

LEYNER

Bro, we're living in the Kali Yuga, a Dark Age of petite bourgeoisie ideology, a petite bourgeoisie ideology whose resources and ruses are infinite and which ubiquitously permeates the world—high culture, low culture, bienpensant media, prestige literature, pop music, commerce, sports, academia, you name it. The only reasonable response to this situation is to maintain an implacable antipathy toward everything. Denounce everyone. Make war against yourself. Guillotine all groveling intellectuals. That said, I think it's important to maintain a cheery disposition. This will hasten the restoration of Paradise. I've memorized this line from André Breton's magnificent homage to Antonin Artaud—"I salute Antonin Artaud for his passionate, heroic negation of everything that causes us to be dead while alive." Given the state of things, that's what we need to be doing, all the time—negating everything that causes us to be dead while alive.

INTERVIEWER

What about the stuff that just causes us to be dead?

Exactly. *The Sugar Frosted Nutsack* is the only book where I thoroughly integrate a personal crisis and an aesthetic crisis. On the one hand, there are the societal catastrophes I just mentioned, and, on the other, the stuff I've been undergoing in my own life. Just getting older, health things, losing people you love.

INTERVIEWER

My grandfather always told me, "Don't get old."

LEYNER

Because it ain't good. But then, superimposed and grafted onto that stuff is my enormous trepidation about what audience there might be for what I'm doing, what my relationship to that audience might be, and who I am as a writer.

A certain kind of writer will say, I needed to discover the narrative voice of this book before I could do anything. My problem was prior to that. I felt like I had to discover, invent, concoct, configure the writer.

INTERVIEWER

Your earlier books have a certain amount of swagger. If you tried to simulate it now, I don't think it would work in quite the same way.

LEYNER

My memory of writing those earlier books was not that they'd been effortless but that I could do no wrong. I had such a feel for the sort of line I was writing—whatever the sensibility was that was producing that language. It was very sensitive and impeccable. Or you can think it's a lot of dreck. But I had a feeling that I was producing an impeccable version of that dreck, whatever it was. And I didn't feel that way going into this book. It's not that I had "lost it," as an athlete would say.

INTERVIEWER

You're a different person.

LEYNER

I'm a different person. And it meant I had to jettison some things that once seemed fundamental to me. The whole stage-diving thing I used to do. I used to say to people, We're all in this together. I'm making books out of a consensual world. Whereas *Nutsack* comes from an isolated, alienated place. This is something I probably would have bristled at years ago, but I think it gives this book a kind of humanity that wasn't in anything else I'd written.

WAITER

How is everything, guys?

LEYNER

I think we're good.

INTERVIEWER

What about the influence of your family?

LEYNER

One of my grandmothers was a great book lover and an enormous admirer, in sort of a religious way, of writers. She also did a great impression from the movie *Pride of the Marines*. John Garfield is in it. This is one of those funny things that haunted me that's part of the store of haunting things I constantly reach for when I think I've nothing to type. There's a scene in the movie where the Marines are fighting the Japanese, and they're hunkered down in some jungle, and there's a woman's voice, I don't know if it was Tokyo Rose or an actual flesh-and-blood woman somewhere near them. She'd say, "Marines, tonight you die. Marines, tonight you die." My grandmother could do a great impersonation of that woman, and sometimes she'd be feeding me oatmeal in the morning or putting me to bed, and I'd say, Nanna, do the tonight-you-die thing, and she'd do it for me. I'd fall asleep to her beautiful little voice, "Marines, tonight you die." Oh thanks, Nanna. Then, I'd just fall off to sleep.*

INTERVIEWER

That could be at the core of everything. Were there other family members who fired your imagination that way?

---

* In the film, it is the Japanese soldiers who cry out "Tonight you die" to their American enemies, a fact which surprises and delights Leyner, when he is apprised of it.

Each and every one. Both of my grandfathers were dandies. One of them had gone to law school but was a kind of entrepreneur. He was always very well dressed. Even when he was casual, he would wear a polo shirt with a very nice jacket and slacks, as you called nice pants. He had a cane he'd walk

In character from *Tooth Imprints on a Corn Dog*, 1996. "My shit has to be sufficiently carnivalesque."

with sometimes. Like Bat Masterson, I thought. My other grandfather, for a lot of my childhood, had a men's clothing store in Jersey City. It was called Ricky's of Hollywood. Now, there's no Ricky in my family, and this was as far from Hollywood as you could possibly get. If you ask me to list my progenitors, Ricky's of Hollywood is more literarily progenerative than literature to me. The patently absurd fiction-making—and no one ever questioned it! Because it was axiomatically brilliant—that's a great name for a men's store in Jersey City, Ricky's of Hollywood.

Did that come from a need for reinvention?

I think the need for reinvention was an ongoing, ubiquitous maneuver on the part of almost everyone in my family, because no man I knew was particularly interested in recapitulating the shtetl life or any version of that. They wanted to be successful American guys. That other grandfather, the lawyer, was a militant Anglophile. When I first started shaving, he was very curious about what blades I used. He said the only kind of blades I should use were Wilkinson. He was like that about everything. Shoes had to be a special sort of English shoes. And he would rolls his *r*'s. This was the time when you could get on the phone and talk to an operator and ask for a certain exchange, which I think he just did to browbeat other people. He would get on and he would say, Madame, I'd like Henderson 3-3563. This is just some Estonian guy who basically lived in Jersey City all his life. There's no geographical justification for any of this Anglophile *r* rolling at all. So I loved it.

Did your family have literary opinions?

My parents were aware of things like the Beats and writers like Burroughs and Henry Miller. I think my grandparents were proud that I had a column in the school paper and that I was writing poetry. I had a poem published in *Rolling Stone* when I was eighteen. It was a poem about Tina Turner.

You published a poem about Tina Turner in *Rolling Stone*?

What I wrote would have been fairly inconsequential to my grandparents, but they were very proud of me. Still, they didn't think that writing was a particularly good life, and they turned out to be right. They were right. I never had any practical, vocational aspirations. They were only obsessional. I wanted to be a Beatle. I wanted to be a baseball player. That was really the main one. For many years, I'd come home from school and get my base-ball glove and a tennis ball. At this point, we lived in West Orange, so we had a driveway, and the garage door was sectioned off into squares. Let's say there were nine squares. The middle square would be the strike zone. I would pitch until it was dark. I would eat dinner and then come out and do it more, always with this chatter in my head of the game, but it got more and more complicated. I would start pitching a game, and a story would emerge of whomever I was being.

I've always had a very fluid, multiple sense of who I am. It never felt like a clearly unitary person was in charge. It's not completely up for grabs. I have some control over it.

INTERVIEWER

And is there a particular sense of who you are that you require to write?

LEYNER

Feeling beleaguered and heretical and persecuted and embattled is where I'm comfortable starting.

INTERVIEWER

Your work certainly makes fun of some sacred cows, but it makes people uncomfortable also because it dismantles certain clichés concerning litera-ture, how books should be approached, how we ought to talk about novels.

LEYNER

I'm really after keeping the reader in a heightened state of vigilance, like some kind of animal in a field who senses a hawk, where all the senses are really keyed, most hyperacute, because I think that's a condition that will make that reader most—I was going to say vulnerable, but again that's just my fascistic, aggressive personality—most wonderfully suscep-tible to what I'm going to do. That's what I want as a reader, or watching a movie or hearing music. Now, it seems to me the best way to do this is to ensure that the reader doesn't know quite what they're confronting.

INTERVIEWER

You mean, you don't want to write prose that's not full-on—

That's not full-on, full-on... I was going to use my name but that's horrible. Full-on Leyner. "Leyner stuff."

INTERVIEWER

You write a lot of Leyner stuff.

LEYNER

If you look over my work, over my lifetime, there's a lot of Leyner there. You know that movie where Keith Richards is making a Chuck Berry birthday concert, *Hail! Hail! Rock 'n' Roll*? There's actually this funny story that Bruce Springsteen tells. Springsteen's one of these guys, kind of like Jonathan Franzen, that normally you think wouldn't be that funny. Feel however you feel about that. But Springsteen tells this story about how Chuck Berry travels around and will just show up at a venue expecting that there'll be a backing band for him. He doesn't have one of his own. He just has his guitar, he goes to the place, he gets his check first—which he said was *key*—and so Chuck Berry arrives in College Park, Maryland, and Springsteen, who I guess was head honcho of the few guys who were the backup band, says to him, Chuck, man, what are we playing tonight? And Chuck says, Chuck Berry songs.

I just want to write Mark Leyner books, you know?

INTERVIEWER

Here's one. [*Shows Leyner an old copy of* My Cousin, My Gastroenterologist.] Nice author photo.

LEYNER

Look at that, before the ravages of modern life.

INTERVIEWER

You still look younger than your age. You're one of those people.

LEYNER

Yeah, but I'll just drop dead suddenly. And they're going to say, But he looked great!

Great blurbs, too. There's a fantastic one from David Foster Wallace—"*My Cousin, My Gastroenterologist* will blow away your expectation of what late-model literature has to be. Unified by obsessions too eerie not to be real, this gorgeous rearrangement of our century's mental furniture is testimony to a new talent of Burroughs/Coover/Acker scale."

LEYNER

Oh, look! If you hadn't shown me that I wouldn't have remembered that he did that.

INTERVIEWER

Later, in "E Unibus Pluram," he wrote at length about *My Cousin, My Gastroenterologist*. He quoted you extensively and, it seemed, with grudging admiration, but emerged with the verdict that your work was "amazing" but "forgettable," calling the book "extremely witty, erudite, extremely high-quality prose television." I heard he apologized for what he wrote in the essay.

LEYNER

He apologized, but not for the essay. David wanted to have a kind of epistolary exchange about these issues, about the objections he had to what I was writing. And I didn't. I demurred. I said I would rather just do my work. This was an amicable conversation. I just told him that this—my writing—was the most precise and thorough way I could respond to him. And he sort of accepted that, I think. What he apologized for was calling me the Antichrist [*laughs*]. In the *Times Magazine*.

INTERVIEWER

But what about all the stuff he says in the essay?

LEYNER

Well, I don't know. He's not here to ask. When he apologized for the Antichrist thing, I said, Don't be silly. When the day comes that *I* mind being called the Antichrist, I'll pack it up.

And yet you claim you're the best father in the world. I remember that some-one once asked me, Do you think having kids will change your writing? And I said, Boy I hope so. Mostly because if it didn't then what kind of desensi-tized human am I?

You guys need a dessert menu or anything?

No.

I'm okay.

I would say it invariably makes you a more generous person when you have a child. Whom you love in a way that you've never experienced before. That changes you, or distills, magnifies whatever is dormant in you that's loving. To what degree that changes your work I don't know.

I don't know, either. There was some kind of shift, from feeling only like a son to this other thing.

Yes, but I would say—not that you're asking such a dumbass, simplistic question—

I didn't ask a question!

Listen, you haven't asked one single dumbass, simplistic question this entire lunch. I would say that getting older has probably been the more signifi-cant thing than having a kid. Having a kid in a way feels like what all the other kids are doing. Everybody's having kids. And you love this person more than you could have thought you could love anything. But you have loved things before, it's not a completely alien feeling. There are other things that happen to you as you get older that are stunning, that shake you up. All the rude, shuddering intimations of mortality. Seeing people get sick, dealing with certain kinds of illnesses or accidents, or just the tension of being a certain age and being wary about the results of tests, and your parents getting much older, and naturally losing friends to various things along the way. I think the impact of those things appears in *The Sugar Frosted Nutsack*. I think, for the first time in my books, a certain range of common human tribulations appears. In a very honest way, for the first time.

INTERVIEWER

I would agree with that.

LEYNER

Having a kid was a wonderful thing, and it does make you feel like an adult. I thought when I was younger that fucking would make me feel like an adult. And it did, to a degree. But not really. And having a child does. You've then done something, pretty much everything, that your parents have done. They don't have anything on you. That's what you think, but then they do. Which is getting older and facing death. I mean, I'm not a man of honor yet. I haven't faced my own death yet with that proximity. But those things begin to seep into your—not seep, really, just kind of rupture your life, and they do affect your work as an artist. How old are you?

INTERVIEWER

I'm forty-four.

LEYNER

So, what … oh, I was going to ask you a question. What are you thinking?

INTERVIEWER

What am I thinking? I was waiting for your question.

LEYNER

We were like family for a minute there. It was like, I wonder what he's thinking.

INTERVIEWER

What's up with him?

LEYNER

I wonder what's up with this guy.

INTERVIEWER

I can't take it when he does this.

LEYNER

I was just talking.

INTERVIEWER

That's all he does, he just does that.

LEYNER

He just sits there, doing that. What does he expect me to do? And then he gets mad when I ask him, What's up with you?

INTERVIEWER

Being a father, did that affect your decision to write for Hollywood?

LEYNER

I was trying to make money. Whenever I went to Los Angeles, I'd feel like one of these guys who has to go work on one of those deep-sea things so he can send money back. I missed my family terribly. I still miss Gaby. She's eighteen now. And when she was a little girl I really didn't like being away. But when I'm gone I want her to have that feeling like John Gotti's daughter, who said, "My father is the last of the Mohicans." When John Gotti's daughter said that, I said, You know, Gabs—that's how I want you to feel about me. There's nothing like having a daughter, to love everything you do. The way I behave, the way I maneuver myself in the world, I think Gaby sees it as unique. And it is.

But this leads back into the question of why I haven't done things that would have been easier, like teaching, because it hasn't been easy for me with money. Writing the sort of work that I write, it's been hard to make a living.

INTERVIEWER

No, you can't expect to make a living that way.

LEYNER

I've been protected in a lot of ways by some kind of naïveté, but it's complicated.

INTERVIEWER

This goes back to the luftmensch/tough-guy divide.

LEYNER

The interview is over, and I feel as if we've just started. We should try some different ways of doing this. We can just go to a quiet place sometime. We can go out and drink drinks. Or whatever else you like to do. We can do that. You can give me different drugs.

INTERVIEWER

I have no hobbies, so…

LEYNER

Give me sodium pentothal.

INTERVIEWER

Tie you down.

LEYNER

Waterboard me. You know, you're funny. I read that recent story. Your shit is funny. Here, turn that off, I was going to say—

INTERVIEWER

I want to record your praise.

No, you— [*Leyner reaches across table, turns off tape recorder.*]

[*There were plans for another in-person session, but certain events, including Hurricane Sandy, which hit Hoboken particularly hard, interrupted them. The interview was concluded by e-mail.*]

INTERVIEWER

I take it the Mussolini idea is no longer a go. What happened?

LEYNER

First of all, I think I was really enamored of the whole breakfast thing, meeting Michael Pietsch for breakfast at a swanky, corporate place near Grand Central Station. It was so totally incongruous for me, because I really do live in my own little world and wander around my house like some Indian sadhu in a wifebeater and plaid sweat pants, so a breakfast meeting, a "power meeting" near Grand Central Station to decide the "subject matter" of one of my books, just seemed so wonderful, so ludicrously uncharacteristic of how I actually go about things, that I was entranced by the whole process for a little while. And Michael's a dear friend and there was some genuine validity to the idea. And I did, for quite a while, wallow in all sorts of Fascist material and make notes, which I added to the mass of notes that I'm always accumulating, which becomes this great festering heap, like some vast garbage dump on the outskirts of Lagos. Anyway, I've always been fascinated by this image of standing on a balcony, gesticulating, and spellbinding a crowd in the piazza below. I've really coveted this image of myself since I was a little boy. It's an abiding fantasy of mine. So I started out being manically enthusiastic about the book and e-mailing people about it and talking it up at bars, et cetera. Then, as is invariable, I started to sour on it with equal fervor. It began to feel too facile, like a sort of one-note épater le bourgeois. And it would involve a considerable political contortion on my part because my animating political impulse is a pure, murderous, Jacobin hatred of aristocrats. I really think that the apogee of political rhetoric was Robespierre and Saint-Just. The Mussolini book was simply too constraining, it made me feel

Leyner in 2011.

claustrophobic, it was insufficiently carnivalesque. And my shit has to be sufficiently carnivalesque. I needed that balcony to somehow detach itself from the building and rise over the piazza and then zoom off to parts unknown. I had a sense of the kinetics of a new book. I wanted something that would hurtle the reader forward or barrage the reader with such a torrent of language that there'd be the sensation of hurtling forward, even though the reader is, of course, perfectly sedentary. If you're a *real* artist (and not just some sycophantic careerist), your writing should be at all times a phenomenology of reading. Writing is, literally, brain surgery. It helps me a lot to think of my readers as shaved, intubated, and catheterized. Anyway, writing a new book involves a whole series of difficult decisions for me. Who's writing it, first of all? I have to invent the writer of the book anew each time. Not the narrator. The *writer*. This machine needs to be engineered, something that, with all its alien hydraulics and algorithms, can think itself into existence. It needs to mangle me like a piece of farm machinery. It eats me alive. I'm a lump in the snake. I love doing this more than anything in the world, but it's a sort of ghastly war waged against myself. This is how it's done: I bring myself to a pitch of crisis and hysteria, then perfect clarity and resolve about how to proceed, which is accompanied by the most exquisite euphoria and grandiosity, and which is then almost immediately followed by total abject disillusionment and self-loathing. And then it's on to the next sentence! So the ideal book is an index of this whole tumultuous illness, this whole garish nightmare of being digested by a machine and then excreted on the side of the highway. So, I abandoned the Mussolini idea and renounced it at bars, et cetera, and then one Sunday morning I had an epiphany (actually an epiphany which was long in gestation) and I decided to write *Gone with the Mind*. *Gone with the Mind* is my autobiography in the form of a first-person-shooter game—well, a sort of hybrid of a first-person-shooter game, racing game, and flight simulation. Because the reader-player is hurtling back through my life as he simultaneously hurtles forward in his, he's buffeted by temporal trajectories coming from every possible direction. It reminds me a bit of that climactic scene in *Throne of Blood* where Toshiro Mifune is impaled by a shitstorm of arrows, except that in *Gone with the Mind*, you're traversed by vectors of time.

The true identity of a book remains incognito to me for a long, long while. So who knows what this will eventually be? Perhaps it will go backward, begining at that breakfast meeting with Pietsch and culminate in utero. You'll have to blast your way back into my mother's womb. Perhaps along the way an incarnation of Mussolini will appear after all. I guarantee that the book (the game) will be mined with leaking implants and secret cysts that confer power. And I think I understand the meaning of the title at least. It means that, borne aloft on my mind, I've "left the building." "Gone fishing." That I'm "out of here." And it may turn out to mean that by the inversion of a single letter—simply by turning one letter upside-down!—a 1939 historical epic starring Clark Gable and Vivien Leigh can be transformed into the story of a little demagogue on a flying balcony.

INTERVIEWER

Last question. At lunch you talked about music with an "immersive, unmodulated intensity" that inspired you as a writer. What music were you referring to?

LEYNER

Off the top of my head: the Rolling Stones' version of "Around and Around" from *12 x 5*, Led Zeppelin's "Black Dog," that amazing Junior Walker song "Shotgun." I'll always remember a particular night in Waltham, Massachusetts, in this little house I lived in with my girlfriend and a couple of other people during my senior year in college, pretty high on weed, so enthralled the first time I seriously heard Thelonious Monk, and then again the first time I saw a video of him playing—the way he hit the keys, the attitude of his body, that whole arcane, sorcerer's dance. Or we could even be talking about a moment when I was just driving around some mall parking lot and Lou Christie's "Lightnin' Strikes" came on the radio. "Lightnin' Strikes" is a terrific example, actually, because it's *insanely* modulated!

Really, in a certain crucial sense, I was undiscerning. I was always more interested in the impact of the total sound as opposed to particular instruments or melody or vocals or solos. And pretty much indifferent to something like virtuosity. I was inspired by music that was about the impact of its gestalt, as they say. As I got older, I started deliberately seeking out music that had that quality for me—Fletcher Henderson, Charles Ives, Moroccan music like the Master Musicians of Jajouka. I took out albums from the library—composers like Karlheinz Stockhausen, La Monte Young, Cecil

Taylor. And of course, I was *very* enthusiastic about punk—the Sex Pistols, the Voidoids, Mars, DNA, all the New York noise and no-wave stuff, and people like John Cale and Glenn Branca. I've always been a huge My Bloody Valentine fan, a huge Sonic Youth fan. And I definitely still have a strong predilection for this whole immersive, total-impact thing. I love hip-hop for the same reason—the amalgamated sound of it, the sum torque of that sound. I'm really keen on Sunn O))) and the Japanese band Boris, and all the original Norwegian black metal, like Burzum and Darkthrone and Mayhem. I love this doom-metal band from Florida called Dark Castle. I've been into Indian classical music lately and Pakistani Sufi music—Abida Parveen, Saieen Zahoor.

Here's something funny, though. Last night, I was listening to the Beatles song "You Can't Do That" and it brought tears to my eyes. I mean, big fat tears rolling down my cheeks. Because I have (and have always had) this helpless, completely homoerotic affinity for the voices of John and Paul. Maybe it's not such a tangent from what I've been talking about. It's the unified quality of that sound that gets to me. Their voices evoke for me this ever-receding paradise, the impossibility of holding on to things you love most, the evanescence of everything, all that—and it's just heartbreakingly beautiful. I remember how people used to bitch about those crazy tapes of the Beatles at Shea Stadium, about how you couldn't hear the music, that all you could hear was the screaming, the screaming of all those thousands of girls. But I've always loved that din especially—that vast, unrelenting din of screaming girls that almost completely overwhelms the sad, beautiful voices of John and Paul. *That's* great. That whole thing for me *is* the real music.

Sizzle Real

———

MARK
LEYNER

NOTES:

Consider mentioning, early on, that Dick Grunstein is the president and cofounder of Millipede Films and that after I script-doctored a zombie movie for him in 2012, we made a blind script deal for a project provisionally entitled Sizzle Reel.

In early 2013, I had an idea for a horror film, albeit an embryonic and very nebulous idea. All I knew for certain was that I wanted the film to begin on a screen at a multiplex. In other words, I wanted to make a polemical declaration of its anti-illusionistic ethos at the very outset. So it would start like this:

INT. EDGEWATER MULTIPLEX CINEMAS
—AFTERNOON

CU of SCREEN:

Wide shot of laughing peasants seated on a long bench next to a freshly ploughed field (à la Brueghel).

> VOICE-OVER
> The earliest known jokes had no punch lines. They simply consisted of a setup. For example: "A man and a woman exit a garden in shame."

CUT TO:

EXT. PIER, HUDSON RIVER, HOBOKEN—AFTERNOON

A bleached-blonde WOMAN in her midfifties struggles with a wheelchair in the trunk of her Civic. Her severely brain-damaged adult son sits in the front seat of the car, spastically wrenching his head from side to side. A small dog yelps in the backseat.

> WOMAN
> (flatly, squinting
> through cigarette smoke)
> Shut up.

CUT TO:

EXT. PIER, HUDSON RIVER, HOBOKEN—MOMENTS LATER

She rolls her son in the wheelchair perilously close to the edge of the pier. It's impossible to tell if he is elated or terrified as he gapes at the river, ablaze with sunlight.

The hollow, breaking voices of adolescent boys flinging chunks of concrete and scrap rebar into the water resound in the near distance.

CUT TO:

MONTAGE:

- Hockey fights, cum shots, Zetas snuff videos.
- Persephone weaving a great tapestry of the universe.
- A hungover Johnny Knoxville in the lobby of the Mercer Hotel.
- Father, in sweat-drenched gray T-shirt, sprinting and propelling a jogging stroller at great speed. Child in stroller—white-knuckle grip on handles, flesh on his face rippling grotesquely like a g-force test pilot.
- Parent telling his rambunctious eight-year-old son that if he doesn't start behaving himself, he'll be transferred to Saudi intelligence, where guards rip the skin off their prisoners.
- Jay Leno trying to feed a dead mouse to an owl.
- Michael Fried: "You don't *look* at a Damien Hirst; you go in and have whatever little trivial frisson that junk generates."
- Josephine the Singer, in Norwegian black-metal corpse paint, singing "I've Gotta Get a Message to You" on *The Voice*.
- Mussolini on his balcony in the Piazza Venezia.

CUT TO:

EXT. A GRISLY TABLEAU OF CARNAGE AND CHARRED RUINS

Shops are shuttered; vans laden with gaunt, traumatized refugees can be seen heading out of town. Detritus of the military's nocturnal onslaught: burned-out vehicles, rubble, melted cookware. A blasted-out armored personnel carrier lies on its side, a pool of blood forming under it. Mangled corpses on the side of the road—eye sockets and mouths sizzling with flies.

An immaculate LITTLE GIRL with pigtails and sunburnt buttocks skips down the road.

LITTLE GIRL
(in cloying singsong)
I've got Dick Grunstein on the line for you. I've got Dick Grunstein on the line for you.

Consider "an immaculate little Asian girl with pigtails and sunburnt buttocks," an image hybridizing the saucy little gamine from the vintage Coppertone ad and the Vietnamese girl burned by napalm in the famous 1972 photograph by Nick Ut, thus implicating the impotent Grunstein's pedophilia and misogyny.

CG animation:

Birth of calf. Vaccination, castration, deworming, and hot-iron branding. Calf weened from mother. Weanling sold to highest bidder at livestock auction market. Grazing on pasture. Transferred to feedlot. Administered growth promoter. In pen feeding on grain. Transported to slaughterhouse. Rendered unconscious by cartridge-fired captive bolt gun to the front of her head. Hung upside down by hind legs and placed on processing line. Carotid artery and jugular vein severed with a knife, causing death through exsanguination. Head and feet removed, viscera separated from heart and lungs. Chilled carcass split through the backbone into a "side" of beef. At meat-processing plant, large section of meat is broken down into individual steaks—

CUT TO:

INT. RESTAURANT

CU of steak on plate.

PULL BACK to reveal Columbia PROFESSOR holding court with graduate students:

PROFESSOR
(as he eats)
I was once involved in this difficult, triangulated situation with two women and I went to see a psychotherapist in Greenwich Village and the first thing he said to me was "Why are you here?"—your basic intake question—and I said something to the effect of "I'm becoming a person I don't want to be; I'm hurting these two women

I care about a great deal, et cetera." And he said, "I think you're being a bit megalomaniacal. You're not the great puppet-master. These are two adult women who are involved with you in a kind of constellation. Everyone's getting something out of this. I wouldn't feel so bad about it." I immediately felt a great burden lifted from my shoulders. Three minutes into therapy and I was cured. I never made another appointment.

Explosion of unrelated laughter from adjoining table.

SMASH CUT TO:

INT. BEDROOM-FURNITURE DISPLAY, IKEA STORE

SUPERIMPOSE: CIA BLACK SITE, WARSAW, POLAND—
FIVE YEARS LATER

A demonic stone gargoyle anally rapes PROFESSOR

as we hear Gucci Mane's "Lemonade" blast from a Bose SoundDock on a night table next to the bed.

FADE OUT

Relatively early in the gestation of the film, I came up with the idea that a character would never just open a door with a key or ring a doorbell and wait for someone to answer; he or she would always use military-grade C-4 plastic explosive to blow the door open. Whether entering a friend's home, a doctor's office, a grocery store, hair salon, yoga studio, et cetera, characters would routinely blow open the doors with C-4. This would lend an antic, lighthearted feel to the film that would play well against the more sadistic gargoyle-on-professor enhanced-interrogation scenes.

I almost immediately recognized that, without my having been consciously aware of it, the film was essentially about my recent bout with prostate cancer. I'd written a scene that begins:

INT. SUMMER PALACE

Tsar Poet weeps into tear pots. Apes trot past. Servant brings silver platter with rat pesto on pre-toast. (Pre-toast is bread put in a toaster just long enough to warm it.)

I was somewhat shocked to realize that "tsar poet," "tear pots," "apes trot," "rat pesto," and "pre-toast" are all anagrams of "prostate"!

But I also realized that the only way I could really explore my feelings about my disease and surgery was through some sort of distancing device. (I'm not disposed to give myself away so fully.) So I contrived a teenage girl—an actress—who's created a fake online profile of a fifty-seven-year-old man with prostate cancer.

I also decided that I wanted to incorporate the recurring motif of Swedish pop star Robyn reciting, offscreen, a very specific line from her song "Dancing on My Own." (Movies are haunted by disembodied voices, by ghosts beyond the frame. The offscreen voice poignantly signals the conspicuousness of absence and evokes the historical displacement of the voice in still photography and, of course, in silent film.)

INT. BATHROOM, NIGHTCLUB, SUNSET BLVD, L.A.—NIGHT

SENECA's wife, POMPEIA PAULINA, sits on the toilet.

CU of her impassive face.

A long beat … then—

She passes gas.

> ROBYN (O.S.)
> I'm right over here. Why can't you see me?

CUT TO:

PUBLIC-SERVICE ANNOUNCEMENT:

JENNIFER LOPEZ

"In the realm of thinking, a painstaking effort to think through still more primally what was primally thought…"

KIRSTEN DUNST

"…is not the absurd wish to revive what is past…"

JESSICA CHASTAIN

"…but rather the sober readiness to be astounded before the coming of the dawn."

CUT TO:

EXT. PASTURE—LATE MORNING

DRUNK KID consoling a COW in an otherwise empty field.

DRUNK KID

You don't like being a cow?

The COW blinks.

DRUNK KID

It could be worse, bro. At least you're out here in the fresh air, in the sun, and you get to graze and shit, eat grass, swat flies. They're serving your cousin at fucking Peter Luger's, man.

The COW blinks. Chews its cud.

CUT TO:

EXT. PASTURE—AFTERNOON

COW

Did you always want to be an audiologist?

CUT TO:

EXT. PASTURE—EVENING

The DRUNK KID and the COW are lying down together in the grass.

COW

(now also drunk)

The coolest reality star by far for a rapper to date would be Abby/
Brittany, the two-headed girl from TLC.

NOTES:

*Consider changing the name of Dick Grunstein's company from Millipede Films
to Ribozyme Films. (I'd just read an article in the journal* Clinical Cancer
Research *about the inhibition of colorectal cancer metastasis to the liver result-
ing from treatment with an anti-Flt-1 ribozyme.)*

INT. GIRL'S BEDROOM, UPSCALE TOWNHOUSE,
MINNEAPOLIS

TIGHT SHOT of ENGLEMAN

ENGLEMAN

You're an "it girl" … Oh yes you are, yes you are. I know you hate to
be pigeonholed, absolutely hate it—am I right?

WIDER ANGLE reveals ENGLEMAN with mentally disabled GIRL
using forearm crutches. She's in her late teens, fair haired.

She nods, smiling coyly.

ENGLEMAN (CONT'D)

It's intangible...

He draws his hand slowly down her back and caresses her ass.

ENGLEMAN (CONT'D)

It's charisma.

She looks blankly at ENGLEMAN.

ENGLEMAN (CONT'D)

You have Fitzsimmons syndrome, don't you?

GIRL
(slow, impaired speech)

I'm Judy.

ENGLEMAN

Mental retardation, spastic paraplegia, palmoplantar hyperkeratosis. Familiar syndrome transmitted as an X-linked trait... Not bad for an amateur, huh? I'm a neurologist by avocation. Some people fly-fish, snorkel... What can I tell ya?

He takes out his metal canister of crystal meth.

ENGLEMAN (CONT'D)

Why don't you try some of this? Have you ever done this before?

She shakes her head slowly back and forth.

ENGLEMAN (CONT'D)

I think your father keeps you a bit sheltered, doesn't he? Well, you're a little slow, sweetheart, and I think this might help. Stimulates the dopamine receptors. Here, put this up near your nose and sniff in like this—

He takes two voracious hits and then puts the canister up to the GIRL's nostril. She sniffs weakly.

                    ENGLEMAN (CONT'D)
     Good job!

She claps.

                    ENGLEMAN (CONT'D)
     Okay, here's what we're gonna do now.

He removes her forearm crutches, sets her in her wheelchair, and wheels her out into the front foyer—

The TEENAGE ACTRESS playing the GIRL somehow slips forward and tumbles out of the wheelchair.

                    TEENAGE ACTRESS
     Shit… I'm sorry!

As she looks up from the floor, she starts LAUGHING, and the entire crew CRACKS UP, and gives her a teasing ovation.

The director calls a short break, and the TEENAGE ACTRESS repairs to her trailer, where she's interviewed by a professor.

                    INTERVIEWER
     Morning routine?

                    TEENAGE ACTRESS
     Wake up. Check my Instagram, Twitter, Tumblr. Then I get up and
     I roll a blunt and burn it down. Shower, get dressed. And then burn
     another blunt down. Drink a Red Bull. Eat some cereal. Then we'll
     usually play Go for a few hours.

INTERVIEWER

Current project?

TEENAGE ACTRESS

Autobiography in the form of a first-person-shooter game/racing game/flight simulator. It starts at a breakfast meeting with my old editor Michael Pietsch (he's now CEO of Hachette Book Group). Feeling neglected because he seems preoccupied with editing another posthumous novel by David Foster Wallace, I commit suicide in the men's room. My ghost has to travel back in time, revisit each transformative event in my life, and execute or otherwise degrade or disable the central dramatis personae in order to get to the next (prior) event. The goal of the game is to successfully reach my mother's womb, in which I attempt to unravel or unzip my father's and mother's DNA in the zygote, which will free me from having to eternally repeat this life. I'm ferried from event to event by Mussolini, who pilots a flying balcony. Along the way, he offers counsel and gaming advice à la Krishna in the Bhagavad Gita or Virgil in Dante's *Inferno*. Whereas *The Sugar Frosted Nutsack* was a book about the male figures in my life—the luftmenschen and the shtarkers—this new one, *Gone with the Mind*, will be a book about the female figures. That's why it culminates in my mother's womb.

INTERVIEWER

Ideal last meal?

TEENAGE ACTRESS

Shot of Jack. Heineken. Slice of pizza from Benny's in Hoboken. Del Monte Mandarin Orange Fruit Cup. I might actually go get that right now!

INTERVIEWER

Superstition?

TEENAGE ACTRESS

I can't watch the guy at Subway wrap my sandwich. I have to turn my back.

INTERVIEWER

Bedside accoutrement?

TEENAGE ACTRESS

Photo of my monkey in a little Red Bull cap sitting at the Go board.

INTERVIEWER

Aesthetic?

TEENAGE ACTRESS

Transparency. Overtly demonstrating the conditions of production. Foregrounding of the apparatus. To contest the domain of the expert, in a particularly expert manner; and to contest, in a particularly exceptional and artistic manner, the domain of the exceptional artist. The aleatory dissemination of text in noncompositional arrangements. The coexistence of doubt and hedonism.

INTERVIEWER

Latest purchase?

TEENAGE ACTRESS

A black Mao suit from Anthony Vaccarello.

INTERVIEWER

What are urologists like?

TEENAGE ACTRESS

All the urologists I've ever met exude a certain morbid élan. After all, their beau geste is the digital rectal exam, DRE. I'm so accustomed to the procedure now that I reflexively dropped my pants and bent over the other day at the dentist's office. The hygienist looked at me. "Dude, it's just a cleaning," she said.

Explosion of unrelated laughter from adjoining trailer, which is being used by the actor playing ENGLEMAN.

                    INTERVIEWER
Favorite movie scene?

                   TEENAGE ACTRESS
That scene in *Lake Little Lake* when the old chemically castrated guy played by Ernest Borgnine is on the paddleboat with Shelley Winters, and he looks at her and he smiles, and he says, "You make me feel like a pervert again."

                    INTERVIEWER
How many hours, days, weeks, months in aggregate do you think you spend just chewing gum and sullenly throwing a pink rubber ball against a concrete abutment?

                   TEENAGE ACTRESS
                    (laughing)
Not enough!

INT. GIRL'S BEDROOM, UPSCALE TOWNHOUSE, MINNEAPOLIS

ENGLEMAN removes the GIRL's forearm crutches, sets her in her wheelchair, and wheels her out into the front foyer, directly in front of a surveillance monitor showing the lobby of the building.

TIGHT on MONITOR.

We see doorman, empty lobby, stray tenant, et cetera.

                  ENGLEMAN (CONT'D)
You like watching this? I think it has all the attributes of fine contemporary entertainment—real time, a hint of paranoid dread, low production costs… Okay, honey—here's what I want you to do. As

soon as you see your daddy on that screen, I want you to tell me, okay? I want you to yell out to me, okay? Can you do that?

                    GIRL

Okay.

TRACK with ENGLEMAN as he lights a cigarette, strolls into kitchen, locates espresso machine, and rummages around for beans, grinder, and cups.

                GIRL (CONT'D)

Daddy! Daddy!!

ENGLEMAN hurries back to foyer.

TIGHT on MONITOR.

We see COACH BUERK entering front lobby and exchanging pleasantries with doorman and concierge.

ANGLE BACK on ENGLEMAN wheeling GIRL back into her room.

                  ENGLEMAN

I want you to stay here and be very quiet so I can surprise your daddy. Don't make any noise or it'll ruin the surprise, okay?

TRACK with ENGLEMAN back to front foyer. We hear key in door lock. Door opens. BUERK enters. He's confounded by the sight of ENGLEMAN.

              ENGLEMAN (CONT'D)

Coach Buerk! What are the odds of us running into each other twice in one night like this?

                COACH BUERK

How the hell did you get in here? Judy? Judy?! Where's my daughter?

ENGLEMAN fires an Air Taser at BUERK. The two probes hit BUERK in the chest and deliver fifty thousand volts for about thirty seconds. BUERK crumples to the ground unconscious.

ENGLEMAN methodically breaks BUERK's knees with a ball-peen hammer.

GIRL emerges from room on forearm crutches.

> GIRL
>
> What's the matter with Daddy?

> ENGLEMAN
>
> Your daddy got a little drunk at his party, and I think he fell down.

> GIRL
>
> I want to kiss his head.

BUERK is regaining consciousness and writhing in pain.

> ENGLEMAN
>
> Coach, I need just a minute or two to say good-bye to your daughter and then we really have to get out of here. We have a great deal of work to do back at my place.

> COACH BUERK
> (forcing words through agony)
> Please... Please don't hurt her.

> ENGLEMAN
>
> Coach, you have absolutely nothing to worry about. I don't really go for dumb blondes.

ENGLEMAN leads GIRL back into her room and takes her forearm crutches and wheelchair.

He returns to the front foyer, subdues a momentarily recalcitrant BUERK with a direct Taser discharge, and loads him into the wheelchair.

They depart.

CUT TO:

EXT. EMPTY MALL PARKING LOT, PARAMUS, NJ—DAY

SUPERIMPOSE: TRIBAL TERRITORIES, NORTHERN PAKISTAN
Asked to describe the Rabbi's daughters, the MAN doffs his baseball cap, revealing the sun-spotted flesh of his balding head, and pauses for a moment.

MAN

The second daughter is more beautiful than the first, the third more beautiful than the second, and the first more beautiful than the third.

CUT TO:

MONTAGE:

- A hawk with a kitten in its mouth flies over the Staples Center.
- Time-lapse footage of hair forming a clump in a drain.
- Regurgitated yarn.
- Shit in a ramekin.
- A motorcyclist slaps a magnetized bomb on the side of a car.
- Scale models of the various domiciles of French footwear designer Christian Louboutin and his partner, landscape architect Louis Benech (a home in Paris's 1st arrondissement, a fisherman's cottage in Lisbon, a palace in Aleppo, a houseboat on the Nile, a house in Luxor), all made out of RED TWIZZLERS.
- Superman squeezes a lump of coal in his closed hand until it becomes a diamond.
- Using items purchased from a gas-station vending machine, the PROFESSOR reconstructs the genome of an extinct mammal.
- VARIOUS SHOTS depicting the preening narcissism of many physically repulsive men.

CUT TO:

FLASHBACK:

INT. LITTLE BOY'S BEDROOM—THE MIDDLE OF THE NIGHT

Fast-forwarded security-camera footage of LITTLE BOY sleeping.

Now, slow to normal speed—

> LITTLE BOY'S GRANDMOTHER (O.S.)
> (in taunting Japanese accent)
> Marine, tonight you die! Marine, tonight you die!

CUT BACK TO:

EXT. EMPTY MALL PARKING LOT, PARAMUS, NJ—NIGHT

SUPERIMPOSE: TRIBAL TERRITORIES, NORTHERN PAKISTAN

> VOICE-OVER

Had a long discursive conversation with Dick Grunstein—I suspected he was on some sort of cold medication, actually. He seemed concerned about a final scene that I was contemplating about a man who exits a multiplex with what at first appears to be a red Hindu tilak on his forehead, but which turns out to be from a red-dot laser gun sight. He was worried about sensitivity related to the Aurora *Batman* massacre and the potential downside of alluding even inadvertently to Hindu-Muslim strife in India—especially worrisome considering efforts to expand market access for American films in India, which boasts the fifth largest box-office receipts in the world. He also expressed concern about the potential cost of using a line from the Robyn song "Dancing on My Own." "That alone could eat up the entire budget of the movie," he said. "Richard," I replied, "if the movie ultimately consists in its entirety only of Seneca's wife sitting on a toilet at a club and, after a protracted period of time, farting, and then the disembodied voice of Robyn singing, 'I'm right over here, why can't you see me,' then I'll be happy. I'd be ecstatic with that." "Who do you see for Seneca's wife?"

he asked. "I was thinking of Oh San-ha, who played the secret service agent's fiancé in Kim Jee-woon's *I Saw the Devil*." Dick concurred. He had no intention of playing the role of the money-grubbing, philistine producer, at least not openly. Then he confided in me, almost apologetically, that he'd backed into Pound's *Pisan Cantos* via Hollis Frampton's lecture at the Whitney in '79 and Gertrude Stein's *Stanzas in Meditation* via Ashbery's 1957 essay in *Poetry* magazine. "I tend to carom backward from one thing to another." I assured him that I do pretty much the same thing. "I discovered Shelley via Mick Jagger, when he read 'Adonais' in tribute to Brian Jones at Hyde Park in '69."

FADE OUT

The very first utterance in the current universe was prelapped from the previous universe. This is why the very first utterance was called the "dernier cri." It was not God. God, as the recipient of prayer, is the First Auditor, not the First Speaker.

EXT. PREVIOUS UNIVERSE

An infinitely dense singularity without the dimensions of space or time.

VOICE (O.S., PRELAP)

I haven't felt this good in eons. I feel completely free of anxiety. Seriously, doctor…

CUT TO:

INT. CORONER'S OFFICE, PRESENT UNIVERSE

A severed head floats in a plastic bucket filled with a slurry of icy water.

SEVERED HEAD

…the Damoclean threat of cancer is gone! I can't thank you enough. An enormous burden has been lifted from my shoulders. I don't think I'll ever need to make another appointment with you.

There's a door between this world and the next.

We hear the SIZZLE of a lit fuse leading to a C-4 charge that will blast that door wide open.

FADE TO BLACK

NOTES:

Consider changing title from Sizzle Reel *to* Sizzle Real *to convey the no-nonsense, everyday ontology of the film.*

FADE BACK IN

EXT. EDGEWATER MULTIPLEX CINEMAS—MOMENTS LATER

WIDE ANGLE on a lone patron exiting the lobby through the large glass doors—a stooped, Giacometti-thin man with a black umbrella.

Who is this paradigmatic man who emerges from the multiplex, from this elliptical matinee, squinting in the glare of this paradigmatic day?

Exercising his uncanny ability to discern deep truths in prosaic facts, he is the *grand vivant* of cinema.

Suddenly a RED SPOT appears in the middle of his forehead. Is it a Hindu tilak, the daub of vermilion paste indicative of caste or sect?

Then we have a chilling realization. It is not a tilak. It is the red dot from a LASER GUN SIGHT.

SUPERIMPOSE TEXT CRAWL ON SCREEN:

In answer to the sermons on the NEP preached by Mensheviks and Socialist Revolutionaries, Lenin told the Eleventh Party Congress: "We say in reply: Permit us to put you before a firing squad for saying that. Either you refrain from expressing your views, or, if you insist on expressing your political views publicly in the present circumstances, when our position is far more difficult than it was when the White Guards were directly attacking us, then you will have only yourselves to blame if we treat you as the worst and most pernicious White Guard elements."

Along the periphery of the multiplex parking lot a group of hermits, fugitive serfs, brigands, mystics, and lost children emerge from the forest.

CUT TO:

EXT. BLASTED HEATH

A blind old man, with long, flaring white hair, feels his way with a stick.

ROBYN (O.S.)
I'm right over here, why can't you see me?

BLIND OLD MAN
Antigone?

ROBYN (O.S.)
I'm all messed up.

And elsewhere:

SURGICAL ROBOTS GO WILD AND STALK THE COUNTRYSIDE, TEARING OUT MEN'S PROSTATES!

Ange Mlinko

WINGANDECOIA

Whoso list to hunt it with a camera?
The Carolina parrot is extinct.
Hunted to nothing emerald.

We'll never see its plumage,
which lives only in the image
of psittacines caught on camera

and in Audubon prints;
but what I'd give to hear the *speech* of this prince
of hunted-to-nothing emerald.

Did it lure the colonists inland?
With what speech or song? Gone that song.
A painter on the ship, not camera:

White bade his shallop men sing chanteys
in the dark, but no one emerged
from the forests of maritime emerald.

The birds must have lured them inland:
intelligent Carolina parrot.
Whoso list to hunt it with a camera,

hunted to nothing emerald?

———

The sea surface the gull patrols
is mollified today. Any painter's
palette amounts to a patois.

It must be this painter's Herculean
labor to limn the sky with cerulean
unruled, which the gull patrols.

It disappears into the myrtle and cordgrass.
Islets of beige, sage, and slate
pass less for a system than a patois.

A value assigned to painters' powers
landed White in New World expeditions.
Better gulls than galleons on patrol.

But now, who's the green governor of this?
Fission of English from its nucleus.
Something more than a patois

says *psittacines*. *Pot pot chee.* (Seminole
for "smart bird with the Semibabble.")
Gone all but the sea surface the gull patrols

with a palate that determines its patois.

———

The Spanish mustangs that do roam the coast
from here to the border of Virginia
have a chatoyance about their coats.

The chatoyance of spools of thread in a
stall, row upon row of them per the medina.
The Spanish mustangs that do roam the coast

pawn-swapped through history
from the steppes, from Araby
brought the chatoyance of their coats

to where what is *aqua* turns *equine*:
the whole world seen through two
descendants of Spanish horses, on this coast,

addorsed on a dune, backlit by sunset:
foaming necks rising from the Atlantic,
chatoyance of beach grass like lined coats;

reeds and phragmites a kind of mane.
Legatees of the Spanish Main,
the mustangs that do sheen the coast

with chatoyance of spools in their coats.

—————

That they survived the centuries is a kind of marvel
—so much gone, all our study is fossils:
what's gone becomes our greatest marvel.

Once, among a cabinet of curiosities,
a nobleman displayed a child mummy.
That it survived the centuries was a kind of marvel.

For us there's little magic that remains
except as what has managed to escape us:
what is gone becomes our greatest marvel.

There were *bells from Henry VIII's fool*;
also, *fireflies from Virginia*.
That fireflies survive is a kind of marvel.

A species—a plant will do—newly discovered
not to be extinct after all, makes headlines.
What's gone becomes our greatest marvel.

Gone Raleigh's colony, gone Wyatt's sonnet,
gone *pot pot chee*, the Carolina parrot.
Anything that survives the centuries is a kind of marvel,
though what's gone becomes our greatest marvel.

—————

I am jealous of the *hoc est corpus*
with which a priest transubstantiates a wafer.
Not what's written in horoscopes.

Take the one-and-a-half whorl
that springs from a conch's seedcase.
I am jealous of the *hoc est corpus*.

John Dee brought back black ore
from his Arctic explorations.
In Mortlake, he cast horoscopes.

He brought back Nugumiut: Calichoughe,
who died, and a mother and child, too.
His proof of their existence: *hoc est corpus*.

Egnock and Nutioc preserved in miniature,
not by Dee but by the artist-governor of Virginia.
What use have artists for horoscopes?

Watercolors rendered with white knuckles
the delicacy of the mother-daughter nucleus.
I am jealous of his *hoc est corpus*,

not whorl-counting horoscopes.

———

Governance from a distance, like a star—
Sir "Water" Raleigh (per his accent)
whose mistress gasped *swisser swatter!*

swisser swatter! massaged against a tree.
He sent his people to the *pot pot chee*
and governed from a distance, like a star.

But the psittacines are silent when
—whoso list to hunt—a silver cup is gone.
Up against a tree, *swisser swatter,*

Native Aquascagoc is set on fire.
A silver (*communion!*) cup. Gone the communion:
thanks to governance from a star.

But *stars may fall, nay they must fall*
when they trouble the sphere wherein they abide.
Down upon a block, *swisser swatter,*

they chopped his head. Gone that language,
in truth: all of its pomp and plumage:
governance from a distance, like a star,

and down against the block, *swisser swatter.*

———

It feels emeritus:
As if asterisking alternate endings to this history,
the ghost crab emerges

along a rumpled smorgasbord.
An octave in perfect consonance with itself.
It feels emeritus:

for its presentation
as a ripple in the vision
it is dubbed *ghost*, when dusk emerges.

Meanwhile a whole armada lies offshore.
Here, here, writ the mirrored feet:
it feels emeritus.

Croatoans claimed a ship plied the coast,
searching for the settlers,
ghostly as the crab when it emerges.

Sightings inland. Daughter, granddaughter gone.
Landscape of sage, fawn hair.
It feels emeritus—the very name, the stars—

when, at dusk, a ghost crab emerges.

———

Named for a queen under the sign of Virgo:
the painter's New World grandchild.
In truth, that language is gone.

Legend has it she was turned long ago
into a deer—*whoso list to hunt*—
though named for a queen under the sign of Virgo.

Her dying word was *Dare*, they swear,
when the arrow turned her back into a maid.
In truth, that language is gone.

Under the governance of a poet and a painter,
the experiment faltered.
But the terrain was the queen's, under the sign of Virgo.

Their word and their witness never amounted
to a whorl and a half of what the court commanded.
In truth, their language is gone.

Swisser swatter. Pot pot chee. Hoc est corpus.
I send you postcards from Wingandecoia
under the jurisdiction of a queen, Virgo;

in truth my language gone.

Sandstorm

ADAM
O'FALLON PRICE

At thirty-three—having misspent his twenties dithering and drinking too much—Paul Wakeling was proud of how far he'd come. He was married, a new father, three years sober, and had recently gotten hired on as an adjunct at the Big Local University. He taught two writing classes a week, for a pittance really, but he loved the work and the environment, the stately, serious buildings and the brick campus paths flanked by Victorian-era poplars. It was a heady time, during which he felt both grateful for what he had and determined to achieve more. Every morning, he woke up eager to meet the day and its challenges, and he had even started working out, his boxy torso slowly becoming triangular. He trimmed his habitual hobo's beard and shaved the patch between his thick eyebrows.

His wife, Meredith, an attorney for the oldest law firm in the area, made six and a half times what he did. Her salary had enabled them to buy an old plantation house two blocks from campus. The house dwarfed the other places they'd lived and featured original oak floors, a fireplace, and a bronze historical-site plaque hammered into a pillar on the front porch. Built in 1872. Sometimes in the morning, Paul—who grew up poor in Sandusky, Ohio—would walk outside with his coffee and, as he looked at the gleaming plaque and the splendid neighboring homes, feel a giddy shiver of unreality that this was where he lived.

He didn't kid himself about who was footing the bill. On *his* paycheck, they would be living in one of the dismal apartment complexes off University Drive, taking the bus to work. Yes, it was "their money," but he wasn't delusional about the actual source. Still, he didn't feel emasculated: in his own way, he pulled his share. His paycheck did make a difference, allowed them little luxuries like an espresso machine and satellite radio for the car. Also, he'd talked his younger sister, Beth, into moving down from Ohio to be a live-in nanny for their baby boy, Isaac, which was a huge help. Finally, besides everything else, he worked every day on his novel, the value of which, Meredith agreed, could not be measured in financial terms.

He'd been working on the book for two years, since Meredith had become pregnant. It was provisionally entitled *Biscuit* and was about their son. "About" was insufficient. It was a paean to Isaac, whom Paul loved with an intensity he himself at times found frightening. Biscuit was his nickname for the baby. After work, he would often stand over the crib as the boy (his boy!) took his afternoon nap and feel as though he was drawing power from him, like a time-lapse flower straightening toward the sun. Thus recharged, he would sit down at his desk next to the kitchen and hammer out five hundred more words. And though, at certain low moments, he may have had the occasional passing doubt about the project, he really had no choice. Ever since the first time he saw the tiny, curled fingers, the surprisingly long eyelashes, the face so much like his own, he was in love and wanted to tell the world about it. He'd published before—a book of short stories from a now defunct press—but it seemed irrelevant now. Biscuit and *Biscuit* were his life's work.

HIS SECOND SEMESTER of teaching Intro to Creative Writing, he met Mark Peltz. Peltz was an undergraduate, although old for it, in his late twenties. He had recently gotten out of the army and reenrolled to finish his degree. Paul's students were usually blank-faced babies, mildly interested, at best, in writing their stories about dorm-room romance and smoking weed. Peltz, on the other hand, was an adult, with graying stubble on his chin, short hair grown out a half inch from a high and tight, and an unnervingly intense demeanor. He sat in the middle of the class, in the front row, and paid relentless attention to Paul. His opinions about writers and writing were mature and often intimidating.

One day, a month into the semester, the class was discussing Raymond Carver's "Cathedral," one of Paul's favorite stories. Without raising his hand—he never raised his hand—Peltz said, "Okay, but isn't 'Cathedral' kind of bullshit?"

"How so, Mark?" said Paul.

"I mean, it's the story of a blind man who teaches a guy to see. And the guy who can see is really the blind one."

"Well. Yeah, I guess that's true. It's still a great story though."

"Is it? If one of us turned in a story about a guy taught to really see by a blind man, what would you think?"

"If you turned the story in, or if Raymond Carver turned it in?" The class tittered, suddenly attentive.

Peltz leaned forward in his desk and said, "You haven't read my stuff yet. Let's just say a generic story about the blind man who teaches a guy to see. You'd think it was crap, wouldn't you?"

"But that's the thing," Paul said. "The quality of writing matters. The brilliance of Carver is that he can write that story and get away with it. Because he's a great writer."

Peltz rolled his eyes and made a puffing noise. Paul said, "I take it you disagree."

In a loud monotone, Peltz said, "*He opened the door. He went to the cupboard. There was a bottle of gin in it. He grabbed the bottle. He poured himself a glass. He pulled a chair out from the table. He sat in the chair. He drank the gin. It was warm.*"

The class laughed, louder this time. Paul wiped his sweating palms on his pants and said, "Well, different strokes, I guess. We can't all single-handedly invent a new literary style. I'll look forward to reading your first submission this week." He avoided Peltz's eyes and said, "Now, does anyone else have any thoughts about why the narrator doesn't want to meet Robert?"

Walking home after class, he felt a hand on his shoulder. He turned to see Peltz, and the anger he'd tamped down earlier instantly resurfaced. "Yes?"

Peltz said, "Listen, I'm sorry about all that."

"It's fine."

"No, it was shitty." Peltz looked at the ground as he spoke, and Paul felt his shoulders relax.

"Really, Mark, it's no big deal. You're entitled to your opinion." They exited campus and walked along a narrow sidewalk. Paul turned left, down his street, and Peltz followed him. It was a cold February day, as cold as it got in the South, which seemed almost springlike to Paul. His earliest memory was looking up at a snowdrift covering the window of their first-floor apartment. Two undergrad girls trudged by in brightly colored galoshes and fur-lined parkas.

Peltz said, "I just really give a shit about it, you know? I love reading great writing and I want to be great myself. I want all writing to be great. And I think when you really give a shit about something, all bets are off. Like, I doubt Shakespeare walked around worrying about hurting people's feelings."

"Actually, by historical accounts Shakespeare worried a lot about people's feelings, if they had money and could provide patronage."

"You know what I mean. If you want to be great at something, you have to be ruthless. To yourself and everyone else." The rhetoric had a vaguely adolescent ring to Paul's ears—it reminded him of feverish nights spent talking to his best friend, Ryan, in high school. The primacy of art and the will to creative power and blah blah. But the look in Peltz's eyes as he glanced over was stone serious and adult. He reminded himself that this was a guy who'd served two tours in Afghanistan—who might have killed people, or at least seen people die.

"Yeah, I know what you mean."

Peltz said, "Hey, you want to get a beer or something? You ever been to the Library?" The Library was a dungeon close to campus that sold Natural Light draft for a quarter. Although going there with Peltz sounded repellent, Paul was conscious of craving a beer for the first time in years. He said, "Maybe some other time, okay? I've got to take care of my son."

"Oh, congratulations. What's his name?"

"Isaac. I'm writing a book about him." He immediately wondered why he'd mentioned it.

"No shit. I'd like to read that. This your place?" They had stopped walking in front of Paul's house. Paul had his keys out and one foot on the first step up to the porch. Peltz stood there smiling, as if waiting to be asked in.

Paul said, "Yeah. Looking forward to your story on Friday."

"Okay, cool."

Paul walked up the stairs and let the door shut behind him. He had an odd feeling that Peltz might still be on the sidewalk, smiling up at the house. But when he peeked through the living-room curtains, no one was there.

SATURDAY NIGHT, stretched out on their sectional, with Meredith beside him on the chaise longue with Isaac, he read Peltz's story "Sandstorm." Then he read it again, with a mounting sense of dismay. The story was really, really good. Not just good, but assertively, ostentatiously good. Fucking good, as Peltz would have said.

The beginning was unpromising. Predictably, it was set in an army base in the desert and featured a protagonist suspiciously like Peltz, even down to the physical description; Paul had initially flipped the pages expecting a climactic battle scene, a PTSD-fraught homecoming, and the usual war-story tropes of valor and sacrifice. Instead, the story was about a group of soldiers stuck in a tent during a sandstorm. *The space grew darker and darker,* Peltz wrote, *until their shadows disappeared, and it was as though they had become shadows themselves, thrown against the canvas walls by something terrible in their midst.*

This sense of nebulous dread intensified over the course of the story; the third time through, Paul understood what Peltz was doing. He was creating, for the reader, the atmosphere that war creates—the itchy feeling that every moment could be your last. He put the pages down.

"Good story?" said Meredith. "You've been awfully quiet." She was used to a sound track of constant sighs punctuated by hushed groans as he read his students' stories.

"It's okay," he said, and went to the kitchen for a glass of water. As he did, he passed his work area, with its pile of printed-out pages, index cards taped to the wall, books stacked on top of one another in several small towers. He was slogging his way through a second draft of *Biscuit,* having gotten notes back from his agent, Stan, a month earlier. Stan had called soon after the notes arrived and asked Paul if he'd had a chance to look at them.

"Yeah, I have."

"Well?"

"I mean, a lot of them are fine, but I don't think I can 'change the primary focus,' like you said."

"It's about a baby."

"I know what it's about. You might as well criticize *Moby-Dick* for being about a whale. Not that I'm comparing myself to Melville."

"I'm skeptical, Paul."

"Don't I remember you saying the most important thing is to follow your heart? How often you get sent soulless, market-driven dreck?"

"Yes, absolutely."

"Well, that's what I'm doing here, man. You've got to have some faith in me."

"Okay," Stan had said, sighing into the receiver. "No, you're right, I do have faith."

Now, looking down at the stack of papers, handwritten notes made in the margins with his cramped hand, he felt his own faith shaken by Peltz's story. It wasn't that he'd ever thought he was the best writer in the world. He knew his own limitations; he wasn't a thoroughbred, like a couple of people who'd been in his M.F.A. program. (One in particular, a girl named Selena, had been able to—infuriatingly—crank out a credible, twenty-page story in the space of a few hours.) He'd come to think of himself instead as a dray horse, the type who gets the work done through sheer plodding determination. Nonetheless, he was proud of the level of quiet craft and feeling he'd achieved in his novel. Now he wasn't so sure. He returned to the sofa, skimmed and marked up the other student submission, and went to bed.

The following evening, on Sunday, he and Beth cooked dinner while Meredith played with Isaac in the living room. Over the last year, this had become their traditional Sunday night. He enjoyed cooking, and Meredith was so busy during the week that it was nice to give her a little time alone with the boy. Occasionally, one of Isaac's yelps was audible over the music Beth played in the kitchen.

It was usually Paul's favorite time of the week, but he'd slept badly and was irritable and distracted. Without thinking, he grabbed a burning hot pan full of green beans and yanked his hand away, spilling them everywhere.

"Goddammit!" he yelled. Beth turned, wide-eyed.

"I just took that out of the oven," she said, picking beans off the floor.

He ran his hand under cold water. He could see a line of white blisters already forming. He said, "That's great, Beth, thanks for the heads-up."

She glared up at him from a crouching position. At times, she looked unsettlingly like their mother—small brown eyes, puffy pale skin, fine hair, and thin lips, now pursed in anger. "What crawled up your ass today?"

Meredith walked in, holding Isaac on her hip, and said, "What's going on in here?"

"Nothing," he said. His wife was three years older than him, and tall, with dark hair and almond eyes that narrowed when she was displeased. He felt slightly cowed by her at times. Isaac whimpered, a precursor to full-blown tears.

"Great," she said, "Now he's upset."

"Just go back and relax," he said, "It'll be a few minutes." She walked away, and he and Beth cleaned up the mess in silence. Paul got more beans from the fridge and snapped the ends off into the garbage can. Beth scrubbed out the pan and put it back on the counter. He had the unpleasant sense of being in a class-critiquing tableau from a Victorian novel: brother and sister scullions in the kitchen, preparing dinner for the lady of the manor and the young master. Meredith had always had a regal way about her, and it was something he usually liked. This slightly imperious bearing served her well, he knew, in her job; when she told someone to do something, they did it. But now, bringing out the food and eating, he felt diminished in her presence. Isaac seemed to leer at him with lordly amusement from his wife's lap. Paul claimed a headache and got in bed early, right after dinner, ready for the weekend to be over.

TWO DAYS LATER, they workshopped Peltz's story. The class pulled their desks in a circle, and Paul and Peltz sat across from each other. Peltz had clearly dressed up for the occasion, forgoing his usual jeans and T-shirt for corduroys and a candy-striped button-down. The students were supposed to go around the circle giving comments: first supportive, then critical. One by one they gushed about the story and confessed they really had nothing critical to say. Of course there were critical things to say, Paul thought, there always were. Peltz bent over his binder, jotting notes down. Paul imagined him writing, You are great, you are great, you are great.

When it was finally his turn to speak, Paul cleared his throat, and said, "I agree with a lot of what's already been said. The writing is really solid. The prose is clean. The character of Dennis is well drawn and three-dimensional. Almost seems like someone I know." Peltz glanced up at him. Paul went on: "My main problem with this piece is that nothing happens. It's all well and good to paint an evocative portrait of a certain place and time. That's great, but there's a reason they call it 'painting.' What happens in this story? Nothing, really. A bunch of soldiers sit around in a tent. It's portraiture."

Edith, a mousy girl who rarely talked, raised her hand and said, "But Mr. Wakeling, things do happen."

"Such as?"

"I mean, they're small things. But when Dennis thinks there's something in the tent with them, it's really scary." Several students nodded in agreement. She said, "I feel like that's just as dramatic as soldiers shooting at each other or whatever."

"Yes, he did a good job of creating tension, Edith, I agree. But what I'm saying is there's no plot. There's plenty of tension in *The Scream*, by Munch, but that doesn't make it a story." Looking around the circle, at the impassive faces of his students, he had the sense of delivering the closing argument of a losing case.

A voluble, doofusy kid named Dryden shook his head and said, "I don't know. I thought it was creepy. In a good way, like it got under my skin. I read it right before bed and had trouble going to sleep. No offense, but none of the other stories we've read so far, by like Carver or whoever, made me feel that way."

"Dryden," he sighed, "I agree that it was very atmospheric and spooky at times. My point is only that it really wasn't a story, per se."

Peltz had stopped writing. He said, "Why don't you just say you didn't like it."

"It's not that I didn't like it, Mark."

"I mean, it's fine if you didn't. Like you said, different strokes. But what's this bullshit about how it's not a story? There are characters and something happens. That's a story."

"What happens?"

"You want me to read it out loud to you?"

"I want you to tell me what happens. Paraphrase it."

"A bunch of grunts sit around in a fucking tent in the desert and a sand-storm blows in. They think they're going to die. The main guy gets paranoid and imagines killing the new soldier."

"That's interiority. 'Guys sit in a tent' is not a story."

"It is. It happened to me."

"Just because something happened in real life doesn't mean anything."

"Spoken like someone who nothing has happened to."

Paul looked down at his notes as though the correct response was somewhere on the paper. "I'm sorry, Mark," he said. "It's not really a story, in my opinion."

"Fuck you, in my opinion."

Peltz got up and shoved his desk out of his way. He stood in front of Paul, fists clenched, and Paul put his hands up, certain he was about to get punched. Peltz leaned in very close, an inch or two away from him, staring into Paul's downcast eyes. He spit on the page of notes Paul had typed up.

"Fuck you," Peltz said again and walked out of the room.

The class sat in awkward silence. Dryden gamely tried to salvage a discussion of the other student's story, but the whole enterprise felt ridiculous, and Paul let them leave early. He went directly to the Office of Student Affairs and reported the incident, per university policy, then he walked home in a numb haze and rocked back and forth mechanically on the porch swing. His thoughts were completely disordered, like a box of files dumped on the ground.

But when he went inside, picked Isaac up from his crib, and held him over his shoulder, the baby's warm solidity refuted everything that had happened in class—all stupid ego and pointlessness—and life's cramped complexity seemed clarified into a few worthy first principles: love, provide, be a good person so he will grow up to be a good person as well.

"Hello, Biscuit," he said.

Beth walked past the door and stopped, watching her brother in the half-light of the room. "I just put him down," she whispered.

"It's okay," he said, "He's glad to see me, isn't he? Yes he is." He kissed Isaac on a little spot of eczema on his forehead and lay him back down in his crib, and he gently shut the door behind him. Beth was dressed up, by her standards anyway, in a black skirt and floral blouse. She'd even applied foundation and eye shadow, light-pink lipstick. He said, "Do you have a date or something?"

"Me and a couple of the single moms from Isaac's playgroup are hitting some happy hours. Seeing what the scene's like out there. You don't mind, do you?"

"God, no. I'm glad to see it—go have fun."

"We might even go out dancing," she smiled. "Who knows?"

"That's great," he said, kissing her cheek. He often worried about her dating life, or lack thereof. She inhabited the role of premature old maid too easily, was too content to wear her pajamas all day. He hoped this would become a regular thing.

After she left, he made an espresso, sat down at his computer, and worked for three hours without writing a thing. It was like wading through a swimming pool filled with half-dry cement. He wanted to move in one direction, in any direction, but was stymied at every turn. He looked up the word *stymie* and found that its first definition was the instance in golf wherein an opponent's ball lies directly in front of one's own ball. He sent Peltz an e-mail suggesting they should talk, and returned to staring at the jumble of words that constituted his novel.

Meredith got home at seven, and he gave up and made dinner, a simple spaghetti with garlic sauce. They ate in silence. She said, "Is there something bothering you?"

"I don't know. Yeah, the novel's stuck."

"You'll get unstuck. You always do."

"I guess. But what if it doesn't matter anyway?"

"What do you mean?"

"I mean, is there a point to it? Maybe I'm wasting my time. Maybe I should be spending all that time working a second job, bringing in more money for Isaac. I know taking care of him means something."

Meredith took a sip from her wine and looked at him over the rim. She had two glasses every night, like clockwork. When he'd first quit drinking, she abstained with him. But after a few months, he told her it was okay, that her not ever drinking in front of him made the whole thing seem like a bigger deal than it was. She put the glass down and said, "Paul, I think self-doubt is natural and good. You'd be a hack if you didn't wonder about your ability. But you need to keep in mind how far you've come since we've been together."

"I know."

"It's all a process, figuring out your strengths and weaknesses, always improving. My job's that way, too."

"I know."

"I think you're great, and I think the novel's going to be great."

"Thanks," he said. She craned sideways and kissed him. He was improbably lucky. From the nursery the boy began crying, suddenly awake, and so Paul got up and retrieved Biscuit and they all collapsed together on the living room sofa in a pile, like a litter of dogs in winter.

PELTZ DIDN'T RETURN THE E-MAIL, and he didn't show up for class on Thursday. Paul asked Dryden if he'd heard anything from him.

"Yeah, I ran into him yesterday. He said you'd reported him."

"I had to."

Dryden shrugged. "He said he was done, whatever that means."

After class, Paul went by the registrar's office and got Peltz's student-information sheet. He recognized the address, a miserable student ghetto on University Drive. On the way over, Paul allowed himself to feel the full measure of guilt for what he'd done. Peltz had written a deeply personal, actually good story—probably the first legitimately good story ever workshopped by one of his students—and he'd shit all over it. In a way, it was the nature of workshopping: you looked for flaws and found them. It didn't matter how perfect the piece you brought in was— "The Dead" or "A Good Man Is Hard to Find" would get torn to ribbons. But still, he knew his main job was to encourage his students, to blow gently on whatever little smoldering ember of artistic interest had compelled them to sign up for a writing course in the first place, and in that he had failed.

He pulled into the parking lot of an apartment complex with sodden clapboard facades badly in need of a paint job. Behind the units, plastic deck furniture and hibachis sat on and around patio areas barely big enough to accommodate one person. He knocked on 3C and Peltz opened the door, stripped to the waist and wearing sweatpants with ARMY stenciled down the side. He seemed more muscular than before, a little action figure. His hot breath puffed into the cold air.

"How did you get my address?"

"I asked the registrar."

"That's illegal, isn't it?" The tone wasn't menacing, but it wasn't friendly either.

"Look, can we talk for a second?"

"What about."

"School, your writing."

Peltz scanned the parking lot, as if Paul were setting him up on some kind of candid-camera TV show. "What about it."

"Well, I think dropping out's a mistake. I think you should reenroll."

"They don't let you reenroll once you've quit."

"I can put in a good word. I can talk to the dean of students."

Peltz's expression softened. "Thanks, Mr. Wakeling. I appreciate that."

"It really wouldn't be any trouble."

"Thanks. But you know, this is really the right thing. After that class I got to thinking, What the fuck am I doing here? I know what I'm supposed to be doing. Nothing to do but do it, right?"

"Writing, you mean?"

"What else?"

"Finishing school might help, though. I could even help you look at M.F.A. programs."

"Screw all that," Peltz laughed. "No offense, but that's not me. And anyway, not to sound egotistical, but don't you think I'm good?"

"I think you've got real potential."

"Give me your honest opinion. Between us, not like in class. I understand you need to assert yourself there, show dominance. What I'm asking is, you know a lot of writers. Don't you think I've got it?"

Paul scratched the back of his neck. The heavy wool sweater he wore was hot and itchy, and he had a sudden and intense urge to end the conversation, just walk away. He said, "It?"

"You know what I mean. The goods, do I have them?"

"Why are you asking me this?"

"I don't know, man. I want to hear you say it, for some reason. It matters to me."

Peltz had a look on his face verging on pure innocence—a child guilelessly asking his father for praise. If Paul hadn't known better, he would have thought Peltz was joking, messing with him, but he knew the question was deadly earnest. All he had to do was say yes—tell him he was good, really good, even—and he could go home, problem solved.

"No."

Peltz seemed to crumple into himself, and Paul hurriedly went on, "Like I said, I think you have real potential, and you should reenroll and keep working." And he would have continued, if the door hadn't shut in his face.

He stared at the rain-buckled wood for a moment, unsure what to do. Then he sighed and walked back to his car. That was that. If Peltz couldn't take criticism, there wasn't much he could do about it. Talent was one thing, but persistence and a thick skin counted for as much as anything. He was, he thought, living proof of that.

THE SEMESTER WORE ON. A premature and fleeting March warm spell resulted in the death of a host of flowers, as usual. The students became even more antsy and unengaged, also as usual. Paul forged ahead with the novel, getting an unexpected wind at his back. He finished the draft, printed it out, and began the laborious task of marking up each page. Fifty pages in, he got excited. It was really starting to work. Maybe one more draft, mostly line edits, and it would be in shape to have Stan send around to publishers. He worked later and later after dinner, pushing himself to get through it.

One night, pen in hand, staring at page 243, he heard Beth come in, giggling and whispering. She'd brought several guys home in the past couple of months and had been going out regularly during the week. Too regularly—she often came home heavy lidded, and once even passed out on the sofa, the TV still blaring in the morning. He decided to talk to her about it tomorrow. He didn't want her taking care of Isaac hungover, or still drunk.

"Paul, this is Mark." He looked up to see Peltz standing next to Beth. His crew cut had grown out into a bushy mop, and he wore a white polo shirt. He was even bigger than before; his arms bulged out of the bottom of the sleeves and his thick neck disappeared into the collar like a wooden post driven into the ground. He had a leather satchel slung over his shoulder. Peltz's presence was so unexpected, so incongruous, that Paul couldn't immediately form words. He half stuck his hand out, and Peltz slapped it.

"Good to see you," Peltz said, craning his head around, ostentatiously taking in the place. "Nice house."

"Oh," Beth said, frowning. "You know each other?"

Paul had begun to gather his wits. "Mark used to be in my writing class."

"Really," Beth said.

"I learned a lot," said Peltz.

"Huh." Beth grabbed Peltz's hand. "Well, anyway, I think we're going to go crash." Paul, still befuddled, watched them go. As they walked up the stairs, Peltz looked back at Paul once and then disappeared. Paul put his manuscript down and went to the bedroom, where Meredith lay propped up, reading some legal documents. Isaac's little snore rasped out of the powder-blue baby monitor on the nightstand.

"I thought you were asleep," he said.

"Couldn't. Figured I might as well work."

"Yeah." He sat on the foot of their big bed and looked out the door down the dark hall. Meredith laid the papers on her lap.

"What's wrong?" she said.

"It's weird. You remember that guy I told you about from class?"

"The one you reported who dropped out?"

"Yeah, he's here. Beth brought him home."

"Really," she said. He could see her unemotionally running through a list of scenarios, columns of facts and considerations in her head; he wished he was capable of doing the same. "Do you think you should go talk to him?"

"They're in Beth's room. They seemed like they were having a good time."

She shrugged, "Probably okay, right?"

"Yeah, I don't know."

"Are we dealing with a serial killer here?"

"No. I still don't like it."

He got in bed and stared at the pages of a novel without reading, until Meredith finally said good night and turned the light off. Whether it was paranoid or not, he resolved to stay awake, and he lay still, listening for footsteps or creaking hinges—or worse, creaking bedsprings—but there was nothing besides the usual house sounds, the complaining wood of the 150-year-old floors and walls. Outside, the wind blew in the trees, a sound he usually found relaxing, but which now reminded him of whispering just out of earshot.

Paul spasmed awake, his heart hammering in his throat. Meredith slept on. No sound came from the baby monitor. He got up and walked quickly, his eyes a hot blur of tears, into Isaac's room.

Isaac gazed up at him, bewildered, his big dark irises catching the ambient light of the moon and streetlamp outside. Paul picked the child up and wept and rocked him in his arms for a long time, whispering how much he loved him. Love wasn't a strong enough word. He loved Beth and Meredith. What he felt for his son was something beyond that, ancient and religious. Isaac went back to sleep and Paul returned to their cave-like bedroom, massively soothed, as though he had just rocked himself in his own arms. Biscuit was safe.

BUT *BISCUIT* WAS NOT. It was gone. He sat down with his morning coffee and the manuscript wasn't there. In its place was a stack of papers with a cover sheet that read *Collected Stories*. There was no name, but then, no name was needed. Beth was in the kitchen, heating up Isaac's bottle. She looked tired, bleary.

"Beth, when did Mark leave?"

"I don't know, he was gone when I woke up."

"He stole my novel."

She shook her head. "What an asshole. Don't worry, I'm not bringing him over again."

"Where did you meet, anyway?"

"He introduced himself to me at Finnegan's. Walked right up."

Paul almost told her that Peltz had used her to get to him, but he stopped himself. She looked so fragile bent over the stove top, pale skinned with red-rimmed eyes. Instead, he said, "I'm calling the cops."

"Don't you have it saved on your computer? It's not, like, your only copy."

"Please stop talking, please."

"Fuck you, Paul."

But the woman who answered his call to the police-department hotline had an incensingly similar reaction to Beth's. She asked him if he had the file saved on his computer. He said, "That's not the point. There are important notes written on it. It's also personal property. Is it not theft just because there's not a monetary value or something?"

He could hear shouts in the background. She sighed and said, "Sir, unless you have a real complaint, I'm going to have to let you go. You really want me to send a squad car over to look for some papers?"

"It's a novel," he said, and she hung up.

He drove over to Peltz's, but no one was home, or no one answered the door. He spent the rest of the day in a black mood and woke up the next day feeling the same. In workshop, his students seemed particularly stupid and incurious, and his own voice irritated him. When he came home, Meredith was reading *Snow Crash* and drinking a glass of wine on the sofa, with Isaac lolling around between her legs. She said, "Did you know Beth was quitting?"

"What?"

"She talked to me earlier. Said she's heading back to Columbus in a couple of weeks."

"No shit."

"No."

"Did she say why?"

"Well, she mentioned how different you've been acting."

"What do you mean?"

"Really?" She put the book down. "I mean, it's fine for you to be having a rough patch, but are you that oblivious to your own behavior?"

"What do you mean?"

"You've just been in a rotten funk the last couple of months. It's okay, you're allowed to be. But I think you've been taking it out on Beth."

Paul slumped down in one of the dining-room chairs. He said, "I've been worried about the novel, I guess."

"I know. I told her that. Her mind seems made up, though. So I think we're going to have to look into day care. You'll need to pick up some of the slack, too." She said this as if it was an obvious fact and he had no choice in the matter. "If you came home right after your classes, you could get him by three."

"And now this Mark Peltz bullshit," he said.

Meredith picked up Isaac and swung him by his arms. She said, "You've got to just let it go, honey, move on." Isaac tried to stand and plumped back down onto the sofa.

"Move on? How about you work on something for two years, and lose it, and I'll tell you to move on, okay?"

"But that's not the situation. You haven't lost it. Print another copy."

He walked into the kitchen and grabbed a Coke from the fridge. She called out, "Did you get the car inspected today?" He had not. He had taught and then gone back over to University Drive, where—finding no one home again—he'd sat in the car watching Peltz's door.

"No."

"That was the only thing I asked you to do today."

"I'm sorry, I must have momentarily forgotten I'm your servant."

"Excuse me?" she said.

"You heard me."

"I didn't know you felt like my servant."

He stood next to the dining-room table, clutching the can of soda. Against his better judgment, he said, "And I'm the one oblivious to my behavior. Right."

"Paul, if I were you I'd tread really carefully here." She continued to play with Isaac, as though she were only giving the argument a fraction of her attention.

"Or what?"

"There's no 'or.'"

"Yes, there is. Either I tread carefully *or* something happens. That's implied."

She picked up Isaac, heading toward the nursery, and said, "Or you might say something you end up regretting."

"Why would I regret it?"

"Because you might, later on, realize all the things I do for you. For us. You might feel guilty for saying I treat you like a servant, when in a way, I work for you."

He slammed the door and stormed aimlessly out into the neighborhood. Brown crud, garbage, dead things swirled around inside him. He was a living rebuke to the surrounding loveliness: the big, well-kept houses, the fresh-faced students, the fragrant afternoon spring air itself. All of this easy beauty—which, having distanced himself from ugly, gray Sandusky, with its hard winters and abandoned storefronts, usually made him feel like he'd done something good with his life—now seemed false. No, he thought, that wasn't true. He was the falsity, the wrong piece in this puzzle, wedged in place by the thumb of circumstance. As he walked, he helplessly remembered himself back home, trudging through the black-streaked snow to the corner market to buy bread and beer and menthol cigarettes for his poor, unhappy mother.

His phone rang, and without looking at the number, he answered, saying, "I'm sorry. I'm really sorry. I don't know what's wrong with me."

A voice laughed on the other end. It said, "Maybe I can help."

"Peltz?"

"Yeah. Listen, I read your novel. Why don't you come over and we'll discuss it."

"I'm not discussing shit with you."

Peltz hung up. Paul turned around and returned home, backing the car blind out of the driveway and almost hitting a cyclist. He sped down University Drive, trying to breathe deeply. The apartment parking lot was empty except for one car, as though the entire complex had all gone somewhere together. The front door of 3C was cracked and when he knocked, it opened slightly. He pushed in.

The lights were off in the room, the shades drawn. Peltz sat on a sofa against the wall, shirtless and wearing gym shorts. He was even bigger than he'd appeared when Beth brought him home, and enormous compared to three months earlier. His trapezius muscles bulged over the top of his shoulders like a cloak. The pages of *Biscuit* sat next to him.

"Hey, Paul."

Paul went to grab the pages, but Peltz clamped his hand down on top of them. His eyes looked funny, unfocused. Paul backed away, out of Peltz's immediate range.

"Hold on," Peltz said. "You read my stories?"

"No."

"And you don't want to hear my notes?"

"No."

"Come on, man. Look, I know you're pissed. I would be, too. I was way out of line, I admit it. I wanted to read your book, though. I knew you wouldn't just give it to me."

Paul's eyes had adjusted to the dimness, and he took in the dingy living room. Peltz's sofa, foam bulging through ripped tweed, looked as if it had been dragged off a street corner. An Oriental rug moldered underfoot. A tightly rolled American flag stood at attention in one corner, a dead ficus drooped in the other. Various dumbbells and weight plates surrounded a rusty bench, and that was it for possessions and decor. Paul said, "I think you need help."

Peltz laughed and said, "That's ironic, coming from you."

"What does that mean?"

"Oh man, where do I start?" Peltz picked up the stack of papers and thumbed through them. "I mean, this is a real fucking mess. I read it twice."

"Give it to me."

"In a second." Peltz got up, manuscript in hand, and wandered out of the room. A fridge opened, and he returned with two cans, one of which he handed to Paul.

Paul cracked the beer and drank without even thinking about what he was doing. The familiar creamy sweetness of Budweiser soothed him. He felt resigned to whatever shabby little scene had to play out before he could take his manuscript and leave. Peltz sat back down on the sofa, beer between his legs, and fixed him with a strange look. "I could give you a lot of different notes," he said, "but there's one main thing: stop writing."

"Right, because you're the authority here, Peltz."

"I am, man." Peltz rapped the curled-up manuscript against his palm. "You read my story. It's good, you know it is. The others are, too. I got crates of stories like that. I work sixteen hours a day, every day. I work when I'm eating, work when I'm on the can. Nobody works harder than me. What do you do, fart around in that million-dollar house your wife's paying for? Take espresso breaks and play with your baby? Listen, brother, I'm the real deal. Go home and read the stories I left. You'll see."

He stood as he talked, rearing up to his true size.

"I am the authority between the two of us, and I'm telling you to give it up. Look, I really am sorry for stealing it. And you can hate me if you want, that's fair. But here's the thing: I'm doing you a favor no one else will. Not your family, not your friends, not your wife, not your agent or whoever. They're all lying to you. They won't say what I'm saying, because it's too painful and shitty to tell someone they've wasted half their life. But because they don't want to hurt you, they're going to let you waste the rest of it. How long you been working on this?"

"Two years," Paul heard himself saying.

Peltz shook his head, and said, "Two years. No way. Stop. This thing, it's not even bad. It's nothing. It's about a baby. You love your son. I'm sure that's true, I'm sure you're a good father. But this is just a little puff of steam. I've already forgotten every single word in it."

Holding out the manuscript, Peltz said, "I'm really sorry. You're no fucking good."

PAUL PUT HIS HAND out the car window and let the air buffet it up and down. His mind had been put at ease—Mark Peltz was crazy. As he drove through the lattice of country roads north of their neighborhood, he saw Peltz's bright, mad eyes looking down at him and felt nothing but pity. The poor, spiteful kid. Peltz had tried to get back at him in the cheapest way possible, and for a moment, in that dark cell of an apartment, he'd almost succeeded. That one beer had made Paul groggy, susceptible. But the cool spring wind that whipped through the car's windows had brought him back to his senses. You've been doing this for fifteen years, he thought—you've gone to school for it, published a collection, worked through four drafts of a novel. And you're going to let some lunatic with a chip on his shoulder talk you into quitting? Get real. The whole thing was sad and laughable. *Biscuit* fluttered in the passenger seat and he pictured Peltz's collection, still sitting on his desk. Probably filled with rambling nonsense, though he'd never know. It was going in the trash immediately, and he would never think about Mark Peltz again.

By the time he got home, it was as though he'd shrugged off the last tendrils of a bad dream. The worst part was drinking the beer—Meredith could never find out about it. It had been a total loss of control during a moment of stress and weakness, but it didn't have to mean anything further. He exhaled into his cupped palm, and, detecting nothing, he got out and climbed the porch stairs.

He opened the door and entered, and as he stood in the threshold of his house (his house!), he was nearly overcome with appreciation for everything he had. Beth sat on the sofa with Isaac, bouncing him on her leg. The last sunlight of the day slanted through the bay windows and lit the scene like a painting, some eighteenth-century Dutch portrait of warm, domestic bliss. His family, the house, their possessions: it was all real, and no matter what Mark Peltz thought, it was not in opposition to some bullshit ideal of artistic purity or integrity. He clenched the manuscript pages in his hand. He hadn't sold out, and he wasn't going to stop doing work he knew was important.

Meredith walked into the living room, and he experienced another wash of gratitude. She smiled, like him, lit up by forgiveness and pride. And she too held a stack of papers, which she clenched to her chest with both hands. *Collected Stories*. She had read it and had seen that it was good.

Melcion Mateu

ABYSS

You and I, when we sleep, we're like whales
because fish swim out of my mouth
and you dishevel the seaweed.

We hear the scent of seashells, the oranges of Sóller:
drifting, taken;
without earth that belongs to us belonging to the Earth.

Two Moroccans inhale glue
and the vapor climbs to our bedchamber;
the city throws its lights against the ceiling,

and perhaps there are cops, and perhaps sirens,
and the air is full of ash,
but our night, our night is submarined.

—Translated from the Catalan by Rowan Ricardo Phillips

Musicians Afloat
in the Night Sky

ADELAIDE
DOCX

Later, after his arrest, Vadim Semin was at a loss to explain his actions. It was a perfectly ordinary concert, perhaps not as big or as successful as he'd have liked, but the sort of charity engagement he'd fulfilled dozens of times. He had arrived in New York only late that afternoon, having been held at security in Kiev so long that he had missed his flight. His cousin was a lawyer for an opposition party in Ukraine, which usually meant factoring in an hour's delay, but this time it had taken three. He had barely slept on the plane and in his head it was two o'clock in the morning. From the taxi, he watched expectantly for the skyline but dozed off and awoke to find himself jolting through Midtown traffic.

The concert was at the house of a retired British financier. A maid let him in and took him up to a small, dark library on the first floor. She said that Richard would be up to greet him shortly. Richard, who had spent his career in various banking concerns and government positions, now occupied his retirement promoting literacy in the developing world. He was a small, neat man, whose alert eyes and curved nose made him look like a parrot. He had no great ear for music but had set up the Piano Trust with his wife, Leonora, who had had a brief concert career. She was twenty years his junior, and Richard was enormously proud of her. Vadim had once heard him boast that she had been a pupil—and perhaps slightly more than a pupil—of Rubinstein.

Vadim changed into his concert clothes and then sat on a red velvet chair and glanced at a program. He didn't recall having the photograph taken. Something about it embarrassed him. His broad face was lifted proudly to one side, and his eyes, peering from the high ledge of his cheekbones, seemed to look from a great distance at nothing at all. Glancing over his biography, he wondered whether "the Special School in Donetsk" was an accurate translation—"special" perhaps carried the wrong connotation. They called him a "great Russian pianist." This error no longer surprised him, or the line about his having been "mentored by the great Ivan Shebalin." The image always came to his mind of Vanya Shebalin stretched out on a daybed in the late afternoon, disastrously fat, perpetually refilling a glass of white wine, and berating Vadim for the coarseness of his fingerwork, interpretation, and soul.

"Vadim!" Richard appeared in the doorway, smiling. Vadim got up to greet him, inclining subtly to the right to spare him the worry of guessing which cheek he might kiss.

"I have brought you some champagne, some really fine champagne," Vadim said.

"Thank you," Richard whispered.

Vadim swept the champagne from its plastic bag. As he handed it to Richard, he lifted his head and inhaled deeply through his nostrils, evoking a luxury he hoped transferred to the gift.

"This is really divine. Concentrated, tight, like apples…" He felt the limit of his description. It tasted good to him, but he did not really know more than that.

Richard nodded encouragingly. "Thank you," he said again.

"No, no. It is I who should be thanking you."

"Your name is getting around," Richard said. "We're hoping one of our more eminent trustees will be here this evening. And I was just talking to a man who runs a piano festival in Kraków. Kinowicz … or K something … He seems very well up on your playing." He looked at Vadim's scores lying on the desk. "But I won't disturb you. I'll pop back up and say hello at the intermission." He looked appreciatively at the champagne again and disappeared downstairs.

Vadim went over to his coat and pulled from his pocket a large cookie that he'd meant to have for lunch. He'd played in Poland twice, once at a remote chamber-music festival, and once in a private recital at the house of an aluminum manufacturer. Perhaps this Kinowicz had been present on one of these occasions.

Taking up the program again, he read the long list of places where he had performed. Condensed like this, the towns sounded almost glamorous, obliterating memories of sparsely populated school halls, mills, and churches. There were a few notable venues from after he'd won the UKAP Piano Competition, and some very prestigious ones from gala concerts he'd played as fund-raisers for his cousin's party. He still wore the suit that had been made for these occasions, with its tangerine silk lining.

He turned the page—the Haydn sonata was missing. It was his opening piece, and they had left it off the program. Was this an oversight? An intervention? Without it, the shape of the concert would collapse: he would be starting with Schumann—remote, solipsistic. What could anyone have against the Haydn? He got up to find Richard, but when he reached the top of the stairs he saw that people were already settling into their chairs.

He stood for a moment watching the guests. Richard had joined Leonora at the front door to greet someone. It took Vadim a moment to recognize the conductor Manus Hermann. Richard was always talking about his friendship with Hermann, whom he'd met through Leonora, but the sight of him was somehow shocking. Vadim recalled a Mahler performance in London, presided over by a magnificently handsome figure with thick black hair falling back in velvet kinks from his temples. The man entering now had thin gray hair and seemed to have thickened and shrunk.

"AS WE KNOW BEETHOVEN once to have said, 'Music is the one incorporeal entrance into the higher world of knowledge which comprehends mankind but which mankind cannot comprehend.'" Richard stood at the front and, by the angle of his body, seemed to be addressing the piano. A murmur of agreement arose from the sole occupant of the front row, a plump woman with frizzy red hair. "I know Vadim makes me feel the truth of this whenever he plays, and I hope you can share that with me this evening." He met Vadim's eyes at the back of the hall, and Vadim advanced a little way down the aisle, but Richard started up again.

"It's talent like Vadim's that the Piano Trust wants to carry forward. When Leonora and I set up the Trust we imagined putting on a couple of concerts a year, inviting friends and music lovers to enjoy the extraordinary talent of these young artists. We are fortunate enough to have this space to share with you and this wonderful Steinway picked with the help of one of our great patrons." Here Richard glanced at Hermann in the back row, and some people confusedly turned to look behind them. "But the demand was much greater than we realized. We were inundated with phone calls, letters, recommendations—and musicians simply began turning up. And we don't flatter ourselves that this was entirely because of our scintillating company!" His eyes sought Leonora. "We realized that there simply was nowhere else for them to play."

Vadim tried to think about the Schumann. On the far side of the room he spotted Oleg, a Ukrainian intelligence agent who was occasionally sent to follow him. This had started after the fund-raisers, but it followed no discernible pattern. Oleg seemed to be the only one absorbed in what Richard was saying. Vadim looked up at the ceiling and attempted to breathe his way into the opening measures of the music. Schumann, not Haydn as it should have been. He'd had a piece cut from a concert before. He'd played it anyway and had never been invited back. He felt embarrassed that Oleg should see him playing this badly organized program in front of a sparse, eccentric audience.

He inhaled slowly. He found himself imagining Schumann at the piano, excited, lonely, tired, a faint sweat moldering on his skin, maybe slightly ill. He imagined his undershirt, not quite clean. It suddenly seemed wrong to intrude on such privacy. He stared over at the piano—glossy, big bellied, monstrous.

Richard's expression was now urgent and inward. "Gradually these concerts have taken over our lives," he was saying. "Leonora and I can say they have been far and away the most rewarding thing we have ever done." Vadim noticed Hermann whisper something to Leonora. His hand touched her back and lingered there.

"We're always hearing that classical music is closing itself off, audiences are declining, people are distracted, no one can relate. But that's nonsense. Mozart toured Europe for years looking for work. It was difficult then, it's difficult now. Beethoven was right, of course, music takes us to a higher world, but it is also a job." He hesitated. A look of bewilderment passed over his face and briefly he closed his eyes. "We need to support that—if we think it worthwhile. You are of course supporting it by being here tonight," he smiled, "but I don't need to say how you might further support it. The envelopes are at the back of the hall!"

A few claps arose from the audience. Vadim came forward at last. He nodded, rather than bowed, without quite looking at any of them. Then in a single movement, he turned, slotted himself behind the piano, and began.

STRANGE, UNASSERTIVE, AMBIGUOUS, the Schumann entered the room like a distant memory. Vadim was conscious of the eyes upon him and of distracted, nervous minds. There was a slight tremor in his fingers, and, for a moment, the sound was thinner than he wanted. As the melody tunneled inward, shifting from one remote harmony to another, he felt his way deeper into the keys, as if drawing the sound from the wood. He remembered the pleasurable feel of Richard's piano—its rich bass and viola-like middle, which yielded to a gentle glow in the upper register, at once bright and pliant. Feeling the flutter in his fingers dissipate, he became suspended in the beauty of the sound.

Soon the piece took on an entirely different character. He tried to demonstrate its bright busyness, the skimming of melody over accompaniment. He reached beneath the jolt of the rhythm for a sadness that seemed to carry over from the opening. But he sensed he was losing the audience. The change of mood seemed to have shaken loose their attention. For an instant, he panicked and could only cling to the barest structure of the lines.

Before the next section, he took a far longer pause than the music required. He heard the chink of glasses being set out in an adjacent room. Just to his right a man was sitting in buttoned coat and hat as though he might leave. He saw the reflection of his fingers in the keyboard lid and heard someone whisper a question. He waited for the response and then resumed, anchoring his sound and rhythm in the probing gloom of the inner voices. He felt now that he was playing against the audience—the intense loneliness of the music seeming to work in opposition to them, because of them. He emphasized notes that were merely grazed by each hand so that a mysterious inner melody arose from the surrounding texture. His fingers felt like liquid. For a moment, a broader vision seemed to hover on the fringes of his perception. He almost vanished—melted into it. It fluttered, danced, came close. But he could not grasp it, not quite. And, as he dimly perceived this, he seemed to fall outside the music. He felt it through his body. His fingers—hundreds of sensory nerves—withdrew. He heard a faint squeak in the pedal. Under the lid of the piano he glimpsed Richard's face and thought he saw in it the mild shock of disappointment.

BACK IN THE LIBRARY, Vadim sat holding the score of the Beethoven sonata he was to play in the second half. He felt a strange sense of shame, as though he had dragged a group of tourists to a sacred spot, only to suspect that it wasn't sacred at all. Near his mother's house in Dikanka there had been a shrine containing a mud-spattered Virgin Mary and two orange glowing candles. As a child he'd feared the statue until a school friend picked it up and showed him how light it was. There had been a manufacturer's label on the bottom.

He looked down at the score and ran his finger gently down a small tear in the cover. The guards at the airport had ripped it as they inspected his luggage. An enormous woman with a baton had rifled through his suitcase while her superior questioned him. He'd had to explain the "nature of his trip" so many times that he'd begun to misunderstand it himself. He had not been able to say for sure if he was being paid for his performance. It was a charity concert, he'd told them.

He watched from the window as some of the guests wandered into a small garden at the back. Leonora and Hermann were standing by a table at the far end. Leonora was holding her glass with both hands. Hermann was smoking. Neither one spoke.

Hearing Richard on the stairs, he stood and pretended to look at a small painting on the wall opposite.

"Vadim, that was simply marvelous," Richard said. "I have brought someone to meet you." Behind him was Oleg. "This is Viktor Klikowicz, who directs the festival in Kraków." Vadim looked steadily at Oleg, who offered Vadim his hand.

"I am honored," Vadim murmured, and turned again to the picture. "I was just admiring this…"

"Oh yes, *Musicians Afloat in the Night Sky*. Leonora brought it back for me from Paris for our twentieth wedding anniversary." They all looked at the picture.

"This must be a Chagall," Oleg said, with faint displeasure.

"It's extraordinary," Vadim said. "I have been trying to understand its symbols."

"The two moons," Richard said, pointing at one, then the other. "Such an amazing ghostly yellow. You can see the same color in the face of the horse floating above the violinist." He glanced hopefully at Oleg. "I'll leave you two to enjoy it."

"Interesting piece, the Schumann," Oleg remarked in Ukrainian when Richard had gone. "It's new to your repertoire, isn't it?"

Vadim was surprised by the softness of his voice.

"I haven't played it in a few years." Oleg said nothing. "For me, it's a little fragile in performance. It's so private, it feels almost vulgar to play it in public."

"Yes, I can see you feel that way."

"It took me a while to warm up."

"You need to be careful, Vadim," said Oleg.

Vadim stared.

"You are allowing yourself to become distracted."

"Allowing?" Vadim said.

"You performed so boldly for the judges at UKAP. And won. How long has it been—five years?"

"It maybe depends for whom one is playing."

"Does it?"

"There is a man in the second row here who did not even bother to take off his hat."

They were both silent. Vadim saw that Oleg had one of Richard's envelopes slotted into the program he was holding. "If you'll excuse me, I must get ready," he said. "Perhaps Richard will have you join us for dinner."

Alone again, Vadim stood in the dim light of the library. He felt a chill and pulled his jacket tight. The pastel pinks and blues of the Chagall were the only life in the room, and he was drawn back toward it. He stared at the fluid swoops of color. The picture stirred nothing in him, and yet standing here alone with it, he was struck by the curious privilege of owning such an object, of possessing so directly the material on which the artist had pressed his hand and rested his gaze for so many hours.

THE OPENING FANFARE EXPLODED from his fingers as if he had taken the piece by the scruff of the neck and shaken the chords from it. He threw himself at its reckless rhythms and harmonies, trying to give himself up to its mania and destructiveness, but the result was coldly physical. Only his fingers seemed to be holding the colossus in place, rattling the notes from one end of the keyboard to the other.

As he reached the end of the scherzo, he felt a terrible exhaustion. The clangorous accents sounded out correctly but dryly. He thought with dread of the slow movement that would follow. Already he could remember nothing of the past fifteen minutes. He watched as his fingers swept over the keys. They seemed trapped in this black-and-white matrix like a bird that has flown into a room and cannot find its way out.

He was aware of the busts of composers arranged like custodians at intervals in the alcoves around the room: Wagner, Berlioz, Beethoven, Chopin, Schubert. And the piano—set in the window before magnificent sash curtains. And the paintings covering the walls, like a giant stamp collection. There was an overpowering smell of coats and handbags and heavy perfume. He remembered the hot practice rooms in Donetsk where he'd often practiced these same notes for eight hours straight. The whole endeavor seemed ridiculous. Learning to repeat what so many had been repeating for years. Tapping a piece of wood.

There was a wrong note in the chord under his hands and he was forced to hold it. He lifted his head and breathed in, feeling a mixture of pain and curiosity at the dissonance. He felt revolted by the piece's overweening concern with its own greatness and he experienced a violent resentment toward those who were listening. He resolved to play the final fugue devoid of expression, and as fast as possible.

A LADY WITH HUGE SMUDGES of purple eye makeup was explaining to him her love of Chopin. Did he *play* any Chopin, the woman was asking. Behind him he heard Richard mention another Trust pianist who would be touring Italy next summer. Vadim had met the pianist. He played showily and worthlessly.

He accepted another glass of champagne from a little girl who had been sitting at the back earlier, and Richard put a hand on his shoulder.

"Vadim, you must meet a fan of yours. This is Manus Hermann. He heard you in the finals of UKAP. Slightly grander circumstances than here, of course, and on a much finer instrument!" He turned to Hermann and added, "We've been having terrible problems with the piano recently. The humidity."

"A great pleasure to meet you," Vadim began.

Hermann looked wary and evasive, harried not just by this moment, but years of such moments.

"Manus is a great supporter of our Trust," Richard said. "But it's so rare we get to see him these days."

"I was recently listening to your Shostakovich," Vadim said. "It's exceptionally taut." He was aware of the difficulty of having to select each word in a foreign tongue. "Such great foreboding."

Manus looked perplexed: "Which Shostakovich do you mean?"

For a moment, Vadim wondered if he had misremembered, but a strong image of the CD, with Manus's name in red block type against a Soviet-style background, persisted in his memory. Exhaustion hit him again—he wondered if it was the champagne. He looked at the small folds of fat where Hermann's neck met his collar.

"The fifth symphony."

"Ah yes!" Manus said. "The strings on that recording…" The two men fell silent.

Oleg had reappeared and was standing at the far end of the room. Excusing himself, Vadim picked up two more glasses of champagne from the little girl as he crossed the room.

Oleg stood with the plump red-haired woman who'd sat alone in the front row earlier. They were in front of a colossal painting of a musical scene. "We think this one could be the worst in his collection," Oleg said to Vadim when he joined them. "Do you think any of these figures were actually conceived of together—as a group supposedly aware of one another?"

Vadim looked; a violinist, singer, and horn player gathered round a piano. He wondered whether any music had ever been composed for such an ensemble.

"How did you like my Beethoven?" he asked, handing Oleg one of the glasses of champagne. But before Oleg could answer, the woman turned to him.

"I have never been so touched by that slow movement before," she said. Her eyes seem to grow larger and rounder as she spoke. Vadim felt embarrassed but found himself holding her gaze. He had the strange sensation of his eyes expanding with hers.

"Thank you," he said.

The woman continued to stare as though she were expecting him to say something further.

"Come, let's sit," Oleg said, gesturing toward some chairs behind them. The figures in the painting looked menacing from this angle. Vadim had a sense of the canvas lurching forward, as though it might fall. A glass dropped to the floor in front of him. He watched the shards spin, riveted by their energy. It took him a moment to realize the glass was his own. He bent down to pick up the pieces.

"Careful!" said Oleg.

"It's fine, don't worry," said Vadim, gathering the larger pieces in his hand. Swerving round to scan the floor behind, he stuck out a hand to steady himself and felt a sharp pain. He stood up, examining his palm. A small shard of glass seemed to be embedded there. He tried to squeeze it out but blood welled up and obscured the wound.

"You've cut yourself!" Oleg said. "We should get a brush."

"It's just a scratch," Vadim said, pulling out a handkerchief and wiping the blood away. No one else in the room had noticed.

VADIM WENT BACK UPSTAIRS and washed his hand. He watched the covering of blood disappear to reveal two small cuts. The pain was surprisingly intense. He wondered how to stem the bleeding. He looked in the bathroom cupboard but found nothing except half a packet of indigestion tablets and some dental floss. He ate a few of the tablets and then walked across the hall into a bedroom. The blood was spreading across his hand. He went over to a dresser by the bed and pulled open the top drawer. He took out a pair of black stockings and began to wind them round his palm, tying them in a tight knot. The sheen of the elastic surface resisted the blood. A drop leaked out and fell on the carpet. He rubbed at it with his shoe, but it left a smudge.

He went back to the library to gather his belongings and stood for a moment gripping his hand and looking at the Chagall. He wondered how long the artist had spent on this painting. He reached out and touched it with his nonbloodied fingers, feeling the grain of the canvas and the smooth, claylike surface of the paint.

He walked over to the window, opened it, and stooped to climb out onto a small balcony that led to a fire escape. There was barely enough space to stand on the mud and gravel. A column of ants crawled to and from a nest in the corner. There was an exaggerated pulse in his injured hand. It was almost dark and the air was cool and moist. He could hear the flap of the leaves in a gathering wind. He heard someone walk into the garden and saw that it was Richard, come to get glasses left out by the guests. He watched him examine the contents of an ashtray, toss them into the foliage, then pause a moment, looking up into the sky before going back toward the house.

Vadim nudged the ant's nest gently with his foot. A dusting of soil spilled over the balcony. He saw the evening that lay ahead. A large round table at the French restaurant across the street. Richard worrying over who would sit by whom. The restaurant winding down for the night. The strained toasts to Vadim's "wonderful performance" and to the "distinguished guest." Everyone peeping at the menu, wondering who was paying for what. And then the long wait while the kitchen made sense of their late-night order and the wine sank in. He'd speak passionately about whatever came into his head, while everyone listened, rapt at first, then secretly bored. And then the food would come and appetite would take over until the sense of occasion gradually faded. Everyone would privately begin calculating the distance they had to travel home, while Richard slipped off to take care of the bill.

Vadim climbed back inside. He unzipped his rucksack and squashed his sneakers and sweater to one side. He went back over to the painting, drew it from the wall and smelled it. He thought he could still detect the faint odor of linseed oil. He stroked a thin layer of dust from the top of the frame, and then wedged the picture into his bag, next to his sneakers. It was just starting to rain as he made his way back onto the balcony and down the fire escape.

Three Poems to Amy Winehouse
by Kevin Young

The world is your lawyer.
Pawn-shop pearls.
Hair like telegraph wire.
My body my bed,
unmade. My skin's
my twin, inked

These arms of mine

& already written
like my obit. Bouffant
headstone high.
What doesn't shine?
I have cats for eyes.
For breakfast
my own fist. In black
I dress

They are lonely

in a looking glass.
Or a shot.
I dance like a thought.
Like a lie
I been caught. What
I am is what I'm not—

O how grateful I will be.

Hungry as a hangover.
You know our nails
are the same stuff
as a rattlesnake tail?
Venom cobras cold
through my veins.

I ain't got
seventy days.

I sleep like a storm.
I sing till
I'm warm.
Mortal, my hair coils
above my head. Smile
red as my eyes.
Even snake charmer
hands are holy

I ain't got
seventy days.

& bitten. Snaggle-
toothed, beautiful, blue
as a vein, I can sing
my tail off. A fortnight
later I'll grow
back another.

I ain't got
seventy days.

I'm living on borrowed wine.
Last of the light.
Only I
seem to mind.
I sleep to see
what I might find.

Yes I been black
but when I come back

I want to be anonymous
as America. As famous.
Market my words.
I been treading so long
this water into wine—
why fight? My tongue hurts.
Even with death I flirt.

And if my daddy
thinks I'm fine

I'm in love with the light. How it
spills across all it touches, burns
& blooms. I cave. I parade. I quail.
For somewhere I've set sail,
three sheets to the wind. Don't
tell my mother where I been.

I said No,
No, No.

Letter from
Greenwich Village

VIVIAN
GORNICK

For nearly twenty years now Leonard and I have met once a week for a walk, dinner, and a movie, either in his neighborhood or mine. Except for the two hours in the movie, we hardly ever do anything else but talk. One of us is always saying, Let's get tickets for a play, a concert, a reading, but neither of us ever seems able to arrange an evening in advance of the time we are to meet. The fact is, ours is the most satisfying conversation either of us has, and we can't bear to give it up even for one week.

Why then, one might ask, do we not meet more often than once a week? The problem is, we both have a penchant for the negative. Whatever the circumstance, for each of us the glass is perpetually half-empty. Either he is registering loss, failure, defeat—or I am. We cannot help ourselves.

One night at a party I fell into a disagreement with a friend of ours who is famous for his debating skills. At first, I responded nervously to his every challenge, but soon I found my sea legs and then I stood my ground more successfully than he did. People crowded round me. That was wonderful, they said, wonderful. I turned eagerly to Leonard. "You were nervous," he said.

Another time, I went to Florence with my niece. "How was it?" Leonard asked. "The city was lovely," I said, "my niece is great. You know, it's hard to be with someone twenty-four hours a day for eight days, but we traveled well together, walked miles along the Arno, that river is beautiful." "That *is* sad," Leonard said. "That you found it irritating to be so much with your niece."

A third time, I went to the beach for the weekend. It rained one day, was sunny another. Again, Leonard asked how it had been. "Refreshing," I said. "The rain didn't daunt you," he said.

I remind myself of what *my* voice can sound like. My voice, forever edged in judgment, that also never stops registering the flaw, the absence, the incompleteness. My voice that so often causes Leonard's eyes to flicker and his mouth to tighten.

At the end of an evening together one or the other of us will impulsively suggest that we meet again during the week, but only rarely does the impulse live long enough to be acted upon. We mean it, of course, when we are saying good-bye—want nothing more than to renew the contact immediately—but going up in the elevator to my apartment, I start to feel on my skin the sensory effect of an eveningful of irony and negative judgment. Nothing serious, just surface damage—a thousand tiny pinpricks dotting arms, neck, chest—but somewhere within me, in a place I cannot even name, I begin to shrink from the prospect of feeling it again soon.

A day passes. Then another. I must call Leonard, I say to myself, but repeatedly the hand about to reach for the phone fails to move. He, of course, must be feeling the same, as he doesn't call either. The unacted-upon impulse accumulates into a failure of nerve. Failure of nerve hardens into ennui. When the cycle of mixed feeling, failed nerve, and paralyzed will has run its course, the longing to meet again acquires urgency, and the hand reaching for the phone will complete the action. Leonard and I consider ourselves intimates because our cycle takes only a week to complete.

YESTERDAY, I CAME OUT of the supermarket at the end of my block and, from the side of my eye, registered the beggar who regularly occupies the space in front of the store: a small white guy with a hand perpetually outstretched and a face full of broken blood vessels. "I need something to eat," he was whining as usual. "That's all I want, something to eat, anything you can spare, just something to eat." As I passed him, I heard a voice directly behind me say, "Here, bro. You want something to eat? Here's something to eat." I turned back and saw a short black man with cold eyes standing in front of the beggar, a slice of pizza in his outstretched hand. "Aw, man," the beggar pleaded, "you know what I..." The man's voice went as cold as his eyes. "You say you want something to eat. Here's something to eat," he repeated. "I bought this for you. *Eat it!*" The beggar recoiled visibly. The man standing in front of him turned away and, in a motion of deep disgust, threw the pizza into a wastebasket.

When I got to my building, I couldn't help stopping to tell José, the doorman—I had to tell *someone*—what had just happened. José's eyes widened. When I finished he said, "Oh, Miss Gornick, I know just what y'mean. My father once gave me such a slap for exactly the same thing." Now it was my eyes that widened. "We was at a ball game, and a bum asked me for something to eat. So I bought a hot dog and gave it to him. My dad, he whacked me across the face. 'If you're gonna do a thing,' he said, 'do it right. You don't buy someone a hot dog without you also buying him a soda!'"

I HAVE ALWAYS LIVED IN NEW YORK, but a good part of my life I longed for the city the way someone in a small town would, yearning to arrive at the capital. Growing up in the Bronx was like growing up in a village. From earliest adolescence I knew there was a center of the world and that I was far from it. At the same time, I also knew it was only a subway ride away, downtown in Manhattan. Manhattan was Araby.

At fourteen I began taking that subway ride, walking the length and breadth of the island late in winter, deep in summer. The only difference between me and someone like me from Kansas was that in Kansas one makes the immigrant's lonely leap once and forever, whereas I made many small trips into the city, going home repeatedly for comfort and reassurance, dullness and delay, before attempting the main chance. Down Broadway, up Lexington, across Fifty-Seventh Street, from river to river, through Greenwich

Village, Chelsea, the Lower East Side, plunging down to Wall Street, climbing up to Columbia. I walked these streets for years, excited and expectant, going home each night to the Bronx, where I waited for life to begin.

The way I saw it, the West Side was one long rectangle of apartment houses filled with artists and intellectuals; this richness, mirrored on the East Side by money and social standing, made the city glamorous, and painfully exciting. I could taste in my mouth world, sheer world. All I had to do was get old enough and New York would be mine.

As children, my friends and I would roam the streets of the neighborhood, advancing out as we got older, section by section, until we were little girls trekking across the Bronx as though on a mission to the interior. We used the streets the way children growing up in the country use fields and rivers, mountains and caves: to place ourselves on the map of our world. We walked by the hour. By the time we were twelve we knew instantly when the speech or appearance of anyone coming toward us was the slightest bit off. We knew also that it excited us to know. When something odd happened— and it didn't take much for us to consider something odd, our sense of the norm was strict—we analyzed it for hours afterward.

A high-school friend introduced me to the streets of Upper Manhattan. Here, so many languages and such striking peculiarities in appearance—men in beards, women in black and silver. These were people I could see weren't working class, but what class *were* they? And then there was the hawking in the street! In the Bronx a lone fruit-and-vegetable man might call out, Missus! Fresh tomatoes today! But here, people on the sidewalk were selling watches, radios, books, jewelry—in loud, insistent voices. Not only that, but the men and women passing by got into it with them: "How long'll that watch work? Till I get to the end of the block?" "I know the guy who wrote that book, it isn't worth a dollar." "Where'd ya get that radio? The cops'll be at my door in the morning, right?" So much stir and animation! People who were strangers talking at one another, making each other laugh, cry out, crinkle up with pleasure, flash with anger. It was the boldness of gesture and expression everywhere that so captivated us: the stylish flirtation, the savvy exchange, people sparking witty, exuberant response in one another, in themselves.

In college, another friend walked me down West End Avenue. He told me that in the great stone buildings that lined the street lived musicians and writers, scientists and émigrés, dancers and philosophers. Very soon no trip downtown was complete without a walk on West End from 107th Street to 72nd. For me, the avenue became emblematic. To live here would mean I had arrived. I was a bit confused about whether I'd be the resident artist-intellectual, or be married to him—I couldn't actually see myself signing the lease—but no matter; one way or another, I'd be in the apartment.

In summer we went to the concerts at Lewisohn Stadium, the great amphitheater on the City College campus. These concerts came to an end in the midsixties, but in the late fifties, sitting on those stone bleacher seats July after July, August after August, I knew, I just *knew*, that the men and women all around me lived on West End Avenue. As the orchestra tuned up and the lights dimmed in the soft, starry night, I could feel the whole intelligent audience moving forward as one, yearning toward the music, toward themselves *in* the music: as though the concert were an open-air extension of the context of their lives. And I, just as intelligently, I hoped, leaned forward, too, but I knew that I was only mimicking the movement. I'd not yet earned the right to love the music as they did. Within a few years I began to see it was entirely possible that I never would.

I grew up and moved downtown, but nothing turned out as expected. I went to school, but the degree did not get me an office in Midtown. I married an intellectual, but then quickly got divorced. I began to write, but nobody read me above Fourteenth Street. For me, the doors to the golden company did not open. The glittering enterprise remained at a distance.

AMONG MY FRIENDS, I am known for my indifference to acquisition. People make fun of me because I seem to want nothing; neither do I know the name of anything, nor can I readily differentiate between the fake and the genuine, the classy or the mediocre. It isn't high-minded disinterest, it is rather that things have always sent me into a panic; a peasantlike discomfort with color, texture, abundance—glamour, fun, playfulness—is the cause of my unease. All my life I've made do with less because "stuff" makes me desperate.

Leonard has developed a style of living that seems the direct obverse of my own but, truth to tell, I think is its mirror image. Overflowing with Japanese prints, Indian rugs, eighteenth-century furniture upholstered in velvet, his place feels like a set of museum rooms of which he is the curator. I see that he is filling in the physical surround as desperately as I am not. Yet he's never been at home in his apartment any more than I am in mine; he, too, needs to feel concrete beneath his feet.

FOR ME, NEW YORK, the real New York, always meant Manhattan, but for Leonard, who'd also grown up in the Bronx, it was still the neighborhoods. From the time I first knew him—more than thirty years ago now—he walked the streets as I never had, into Brooklyn, Queens, Staten Island. He knew Sunnyside, Greenpoint, Red Hook, Washington Heights, East Harlem, the South Bronx. He knew the meaning of a shopping street in Queens with half the stores boarded up, a piece of Brooklyn waterfront restored, a garden lot in Harlem full of deranged-looking flowers, a warehouse on the East River converted to a third-world mall. He knew which housing projects worked and which were a devastation. And it wasn't just the streets he knew. He knew the piers, the railroad yards, the subway lines. He had Central Park and Prospect Park by heart. He knew the footbridges on the East River; the ferries, the tunnels, the beltways. He knew Snug Harbor and City Island and Jamaica Bay.

He often reminded me of the street-urchin protagonists in postwar Italian movies: those handsome, ragged children of Rossellini's who imprint on Rome by knowing the city inside out. Leonard always looked like that to me when we took one of our long hikes through the boroughs: hungry, as only a working-class kid can be, for information; the kind of information that makes the ground beneath your feet yours. With him as my guide, the neighborhoods spread out for miles in all directions, often looking to my uninformed eye like wasteland until I began to see them as Leonard did: an incomparable sea of ghettos forever bleeding new life into a rectangle of glamour and prosperity.

On these treks of ours the character of time and space often changed as we walked. The concept of "hours" evaporated. The streets became one long ribbon of open road stretched out before us, with nothing to impede our progress. Time expanded to resemble time in one's childhood, when it seemed never to end, as opposed to time now: always scarce, always pressing, always a marker of one's emotional well-being.

AT A NEW YEAR'S PARTY Jim comes rushing toward me. Sarah nods and turns away. A year ago I was tight with one, two years ago with the other.

Tonight I realize I haven't seen him in three months, her in six. A woman who lives three blocks from me appears, her eyes shimmering. "I miss you!" she breathes wistfully, as though we're lovers in wartime separated by forces beyond our control. Yes, I nod, and move on. We'll embrace happily, me and all these people: not a glance of grievance, not a syllable of reproach among us. And, indeed, there is no call for grievance. Like pieces in a kaleidoscope that's been shaken, we've all simply shifted positions in the pattern of intimate exchange. Many of us who not so long ago were seeing each other regularly, will meet now more often by accident than by design: in a restaurant, on the bus, at a loft wedding. Ah, but here's someone I haven't seen in years. Suddenly, a flare of intensity and we're meeting once a week for the next six months.

I am often reminded of the tenement friendships in my childhood, circumstantial one and all. Round, dark-eyed women, filled with muted understanding for the needs of the moment. What difference did it make if the next-door neighbor was called Ida or Goldie when you needed someone to lend you ten bucks or recommend an abortionist or nod her head during an outburst of marital rage. It mattered only that there was a next-door neighbor. These attachments, as Sartre might have put it, were contingent rather than essential.

As for us: never before in history has so much educated intelligence been expended on the idea of the irreplaceable—the essential—self; and never before has devotion to the slightest amount of psychological discomfort allowed so many to be treated as the contingent other.

MICHEL DE MONTAIGNE DESCRIBES the great friendship of his youth with Étienne de la Boétie as one in which a perfect communion of the spirit made the "soul grow refined." In the 1790s, Samuel Taylor Coleridge worshipped an idea of friendship that embodied the same ideal. Living at a time when persons of sensibility yearned for communion of the spirit, its frequent failure to materialize in friendship made Coleridge suffer, but the pain did not threaten his faith, not even when he lost the friendship that defined all others.

Coleridge and Wordsworth met in 1795 when they were, respectively, twenty-three and twenty-five years old. Wordsworth—grave, thin-skinned, self-protective—was, even then, steadied by an inner conviction of his own coming greatness as a poet; Coleridge, on the other hand—brilliant, explosive, self-doubting to the point of instability—was already into opium. Anyone except them could see that they were bound to come a cropper. In 1795, however, a new world, a new poetry, a new way of being was forming itself, and, at that moment, both Wordsworth and Coleridge, each feeling the newness at work in himself, saw proof of its existence reflected in the person of the other.

The infatuation lasted a little more than a year and a half. At the end of that time, the chaos within Coleridge doubled its dominion; the pride in Wordsworth stiffened into near immobility. The person each had been for nearly two years—the one who had basked in the unbroken delight of the other—was no more. It wasn't exactly that they were returned to the persons they had been before; it was only that never again would either feel his own best self in the presence of the other.

One's own best self. For centuries, this was the key concept behind any essential definition of friendship: that one's friend is a virtuous being who speaks to the virtue in oneself. How foreign is such a concept to the children of the therapeutic culture! Today we do not look to see, much less affirm, our best selves in one another. To the contrary, it is the openness with which we admit to our emotional incapacities—the fear, the anger, the humiliation—that excites contemporary bonds of friendship. Nothing draws us closer to one another than the degree to which we face our deepest shame openly in one another's company. Coleridge and Wordsworth dreaded such self-exposure; we adore it. What we want is to feel *known*, warts and all; the more warts the better. It is the great illusion of our culture that what we confess to is who we are.

EVERY NIGHT WHEN I TURN the lights out in my sixteenth-floor living room before I go to bed, I experience a shock of pleasure as I see the banks of lighted windows rising to the sky, crowding round me, and feel myself embraced by the anonymous ingathering of city dwellers. This swarm of human hives, also hanging anchored in space, is the New York design offering generic connection. The pleasure it gives soothes beyond all explanation.

THE PHONE RINGS. It's Leonard.

"What are you doing?" he asks.

"Reading Krista K.," I reply.

"Who's she?" he asks.

"Who's she!" I say. "She's one of the most famous writers in Eastern Europe."

"Oh," he says matter-of-factly. "What's the book like?"

"A bit claustrophobic," I sigh. "You don't really know where you are most of the time, or who's speaking. Then every twenty pages or so she says, 'Ran into G this morning. Asked him how long he thought we could go on like this. He shrugged. Yes, I said.'"

"Oh," Leonard says. "One of those. Bor-ring."

"Tell me," I say, "don't you ever mind sounding like a Philistine?"

"The Philistines were a much maligned people," he says. "Have you seen Lorenzo lately?"

"No, why?"

"He's drinking again."

"For God's sake! What's wrong now?"

"What's wrong now? What's *right* now? What's ever right for Lorenzo?"

"Can't you talk to him? You know him so well."

"I *do* talk to him. He nods along with me as I speak. I know, I know, he says, you're right, I've got to pull it together, thanks so much for saying this, I'm so grateful, I don't know why I fuck up, I just don't know."

"Why *does* he fuck up?"

"Why? Because if he's not fucking up, he doesn't know who he is."

Leonard's voice has become charged.

"It's unbelievable," he swears on, "the muddle in his mind. I say to him, What do you want, what is it you *want*?"

"Tell me," I cut in, "what do *you* want?"

"Touché," Leonard laughs drily.

There follows a few long seconds of vital silence.

"In my life," he says, "I have known only what I *don't* want. I've always had a thorn in my side, and I've always thought, When this thorn is removed I'll think about what I want. But then that particular thorn would be removed, and I'd be left feeling emptied out. In a short time another thorn would be inserted into my side. Then, once again, all I had to think about was being free of the thorn in my side. I've never had time to think about what I *want*."

"Maybe somewhere in there is a clue to why Lorenzo drinks."

"It's disgusting," Leonard says softly, "to be this old and have so little information. Now, *there's* something Krista K. could write about that would interest me. The only problem is she thinks information is what the KGB was after."

IN THE DRUGSTORE I run into ninety-year-old Vera, a Trotskyist from way back who lives in a fourth-floor walk-up in my neighborhood, and whose voice is always pitched at the level of soapbox urgency. She is waiting for a prescription to be filled, and, as I haven't seen her in a long while, on impulse I offer to wait with her. We sit down in two of the three chairs lined up near the prescription counter, me in the middle, Vera on my left, and on my right a pleasant-looking man reading a book.

"Still living in the same place?" I ask.

"Where'm I gonna go?" she says, loudly enough for a man on the pick-up line to turn in our direction. "But y'know, dolling? The stairs keep me strong."

"And your husband? How's he taking the stairs?"

"Oh, him," she says. "He died."

"I'm so sorry," I murmur.

Her hand pushes away the air.

"It wasn't a good marriage," she announces. Three people on the line turn around. "But, y'know? In the end it doesn't really matter."

I nod my head. I understand. The apartment is empty.

"One thing I gotta say," she goes on, "he was a no-good husband, but he was a great lover."

I can feel a slight jolt in the body of the man sitting beside me.

"Well, that's certainly important," I say.

"Boy, was it ever! I met him in Detroit during the Second World War. We were organizing. In those days, everybody slept with everybody, so I did, too. But you wouldn't believe it"—and here she lowered her voice dramatically, as though she had a secret of some importance to relate—"most of the guys I slept with? They were no good in bed. I mean, they were bad, really *bad*."

Now I feel the man on my right stifling a laugh.

"So when you found a good one," Vera shrugs, "you held onto him."

"I know just what you mean," I say.

"Do you, dolling?"

"Of course I do."

"You mean they're still bad?"

"Listen to us," I say. "Two old women talking about lousy lovers."

This time the man beside me laughs out loud. I turn and look at him.

"We're sleeping with the same guys, right?" I say.

Yes, he nods. "And with the same ratio of satisfaction."

For a split second the three of us look at one another, and then, all at once, we begin to howl. When the howling stops, we are all beaming. Together we have performed, and separately we have been received.

NO ONE IS MORE SURPRISED than I that I turned out to be who I am. Take love, for instance. I had always assumed that, in this regard, I was like every other girl of my generation. While motherhood and marriage had never held my interest, and daydreaming myself on some revolutionary barricade was peculiar among my classmates, I always knew that one day Prince Passion would come along, and when he did, life would assume its ultimate shape; *ultimate* being the operative word. As it happened, a number of PP look-alikes did appear, but there was no ultimate anything. Before I was thirty-five I had been as much bedded as any of my friends, and I had also been twice married, twice divorced. Each marriage lasted two and a half years, and each was undertaken by a woman I didn't know (me) to a man I also didn't know (the figure on the wedding cake).

It was only after these marriages were over that I matured sexually; that is, I became conscious of myself as a person preoccupied with desiring rather than being desired; and *that* development gave me an education. I learned that I was sensual but not a sensualist; that I blissed out on orgasm but the earth didn't move; that I could be strung out on erotic obsession for six months or so but was always waiting for the nervous excitement to die down. In a word: lovemaking was sublime but it wasn't where I lived. And then I learned something more.

In my late thirties I had an affair with a man I cared for and who cared for me. This man and I were both drawn to the energy of mind and spirit that each of us felt in the other. But for this man, too—intelligent, educated, politically passionate as he was—the exercise of his sexual will was central to any connection he made with a woman. There was not a moment when we were together that he wasn't touching me. He never walked into my house that his hand wasn't immediately on my breast; never embraced me that he wasn't reaching for my genitals; never lay beside me that he wasn't trying to make me come. When, after we'd been together some months, I began to object to what had started to feel like an on-automatic practice, he would invariably put his arms around me, nuzzle my neck, and whisper in my ear, "C'mon, you know you like it." As I did genuinely love him and he me—we had memorable times together—I would stare at him at such moments, shake my head in exasperation, but then let it go.

One day, he suggested that I let him sodomize me, something we'd not done before. I demurred. Next day he made the same suggestion. Again, I demurred. "How do you know you won't like it," he persisted, "if you've never done it." He wore me down: I agreed to try it once. No, no, he said, I must agree to do it three times and *then* if I said no it would be no. So we did it three times and, truth to tell, I didn't hate the physical sensation as much as I had thought I would—almost against my will my body responded—but I definitely did not like it. "Okay," I said, "I've done it three times, and I don't want to do it any more." We were lying in bed. He nuzzled my neck and whispered in my ear, "C'mon. Just one more time. You know you like it."

I drew away then and looked directly into his face. "No," I said, and was startled by the finality in my own voice.

"What an unnatural woman you are!" he exploded at me. "You know you want to do it. *I* know you want to do it. Yet you fight it. Or is it me you're fighting?"

Once again, I stared at him: only this stare was different from those other stares. A man was pressing me to do something I did not want to do, and pressing me in a manner he would never have applied to another man: by telling me that I didn't know what I wanted. I felt my eyes narrowing and my heart going cold. For the first—but not the last—time I consciously felt men to be members of a species separate from myself. Separate and foreign. It was as though an invisible membrane had fallen between me and my lover, one fine enough to be penetrated by desire but opaque enough to obscure human fellowship. The person on the other side of the membrane seemed as unreal to me as I felt myself to be to him. At that moment, I didn't care if I never again got into bed with a man.

I did of course get into bed with them—love, quarrel, and bliss out many more times after this man and I parted—but the memory of that fine, invisible separation haunted me; and more often than I like to remember, I saw it glistening as I gazed into the face of a man who loved me but was not persuaded that I needed what he needed to feel like a human being.

In time, I came to know other women who would have analyzed the experience differently but immediately understood what I was talking about when I described the invisible curtain. It comes with the territory, most of them shrugged.

Work, I said to myself, work. If I worked, I thought, pressing myself against my newly hardened heart, I'd have what I needed. I'd be a person in the world. What would it matter then that I was giving up "love"?

As it turned out, it mattered more than I had ever dreamed it would. As the years went on, I saw that romantic love was injected like dye into the nervous system of my emotions, laced through the entire fabric of longing, fantasy, and sentiment. It haunted the psyche, was an ache in the bones; so deeply embedded in the makeup of the spirit it hurt the eyes to look directly into its influence. It would be a cause of pain and conflict for the rest of my life. I prize my hardened heart—I have prized it all these years—but the loss of romantic love can still tear at it.

WORKMEN HAVE ERECTED a wooden barrier on my street around two squares of pavement whose concrete has been newly poured. Beside the barrier is a single wooden plank laid out for pedestrians, and beside that, a flimsy railing. On an icy morning in midwinter I am about to grasp the railing and pull myself along the plank when, at the other end, a man appears, attempting the same negotiation. This man is tall, painfully thin, and fearfully old. Instinctively, I lean in far enough to hold out my hand to him. Instinctively, he grasps it. Neither of us speaks a word until he is safely across the plank, standing beside me. "Thank you," he says. "Thank you very much." A thrill runs through me. "You're welcome," I say, in a tone that I hope is as plain as his. We each then go our separate ways, but I feel that "thank you" running through my veins all the rest of the day.

It was his voice that had done it. That voice! Strong, vibrant, self-possessed: it did not know it belonged to an old man. There was in it not a hint of that beseeching tone one hears so often in the voice of an old person when small courtesies are shown—"You're so kind, so kind, so very kind," when all you're doing is hailing a cab or helping to unload a shopping cart—as though the person is apologizing for the room he or she is taking up in the world. This man realized that I had not been inordinately helpful, and he need not be inordinately thankful. He was recalling for both of us the ordinary recognition that every person in trouble has a right to expect, and every witness an obligation to extend. I had held out my hand, he had taken it. For thirty seconds we had stood together—he not pleading, I not patronizing—the mask of old age slipped from his face, the mask of vigor dropped from mine.

A FEW WEEKS AGO a woman who lives on my floor invited me to a Sunday brunch. This woman has taught grade school for years, but she looks upon teaching as a day job. In *real* life, she says, she is an actor. None of the people at the brunch—all in their forties and fifties—knew each other well, and some didn't know the others at all, but it soon became clear that everyone at the table also thought of the work they did as day jobs; every one of them saw him or herself as having a vocation in the arts, albeit one without material achievement. The chatter on that Sunday morning was animated by one account after another of this or that failed audition or publication or gallery showing, each one ending with "I didn't prepare hard enough," or "I knew I should have rewritten the beginning," or "I don't send out enough slides." What was striking was the sympathy that each self-reproach called to life in the others. "Oh, you're too hard on yourself!" was heard more than once. Then, abruptly, looking directly at the last person to say, "You're too hard on yourself," a woman who'd been silent started to speak.

"When I got divorced," she said, " I had to sell the house in Westchester. A couple in the business of importing Chinese furniture and art objects bought the house and began moving things in a week before I was to leave. One night I went down into the basement and began looking through some of their crates. I found a pair of beautiful porcelain vases. On impulse, I took one. I thought, They've got everything, I've got nothing, why shouldn't I? When I moved, I took the vase with me. A week later the husband called and said this funny thing had happened, one of this pair of vases had disappeared, did I know anything about it. No, I said, sounding as bemused as he, I didn't know anything about it, I'd never even seen the vases. I felt awful then. But I didn't know what to do. I put the vase in a closet and never looked at it again. Ten years passed. Then I began thinking about the vase. Soon the thought of the vase began to obsess me. Finally, this past year I couldn't stand it anymore. I packed up the vase as carefully as I could and sent it back to them. And I wrote a separate letter, saying I didn't know what had possessed me, why I had taken this thing that belonged to them, and I wasn't asking for forgiveness, but here it was back. A few weeks later the wife called me. She said she'd gotten this strange letter from me, she didn't know what I was talking about, and then this package came, and inside the package was about a thousand shards of something or other. What on earth was it that I had taken and was now sending back?"

AT TEN IN THE MORNING, two old women are walking ahead of me on West Twenty-Third Street, one wearing a pink nylon sweater, the other a blue. "Did you hear?" the woman in pink says. "The pope appealed to capitalism to be kind to the poor of the world." The woman in blue responds, "What did capitalism say?" As we're crossing Seventh Avenue, the woman in pink shrugs, "So far it's quiet."

At noon, a man at a grocery counter stands peering at the change in his hand. "You gave me $8.06," he says to the young woman behind the cash register. "I don't think that's right." She looks at the coins and says, "You're right. It shoulda been $8.60," and gives the man the correct change. He continues to stare at his open palm. "You put the six and the zero in the wrong place," he says. "It shoulda been the other way around." Now it's the woman who stares. When at last the man turns away, I shake my head sympathetically. "What I put up with all day long," she sighs, as I pile my purchases on the counter. "Would you believe this? A guy comes up to the counter with an item. It's marked wrong. I can see right away, it's the wrong amount. I tell him, Listen, that's the wrong price. Believe me, I know the prices, I been working in the store two years. He says to me, 'That's nothing to be proud of,' and he marches out."

At three in the afternoon, a distinguished-looking couple is standing under the awning of the Regency Hotel on Park Avenue. The man has iron-gray hair and regular features, and is wearing an expensive overcoat. The woman is alcoholic thin, has blonde, marcelled hair, and is wearing mink. She looks up at him as I pass them, and her face lights up. "It's been a *wonderful* afternoon," she says. The man embraces her warmly and nods directly into her face. The scene excites my own gratitude: how delicious to see people of the upper classes acting with simple humanity! Later I run into Sarah, a tired socialist of my acquaintance, and I tell her about the couple on Park Avenue.

She listens with her customary Marxist moroseness and says, "You think she knows what a wonderful afternoon is?"

A FRIEND READS what I've been writing and says to me over coffee, "You're romanticizing the street. Don't you know that New York has lost seventy-five percent of its manufacturing base?" In my mind's eye I stare into the faces of all the women and men with whom I interact daily. Hey you people, I address them silently, did you hear what my friend just said? The city is doomed, the middle class has deserted New York, the corporations are in Texas, Jersey, Taiwan. You're gone, you're outta here, it's all over. How come you're still on the street?

New York isn't jobs, they reply, it's temperament. Most people are in New York because they need evidence—in large quantities—of human expressiveness; and they need it, not now and then, but every day. That is what they *need*. Those who go off to the manageable cities can do without; those who come to New York cannot.

Or perhaps I should say that it is I who cannot.

IT'S THE VOICES I can't do without. In most cities of the world, the populace is planted in centuries of cobblestoned alleys, ruined churches, architectural relics, none of which are ever dug up, only piled one on top of another. If you've grown up in New York your life is an archaeology not of structures but of voices, also piled one on top of another, also not really replacing one another.

On Sixth Avenue, two small, dark-skinned men lean against a parked cab. One says to the other, "Look, it's very simple. A is the variable costs, B is the gross income, C is the overhead. Got that?" The other man shakes his head no. "Dummy!" the first man cries. "You gotta *get* it!"

On Park Avenue a well-dressed matron says to her friend, "When I was young, men were the main course, now they're a condiment."

On Fifty-Seventh Street a delicate-looking man says to a woman too young to know what he's talking about, "These days my life feels like a chicken bone stuck in my craw. I can't swallow it and I can't cough it up. Right now I'm trying to just not choke on it."

As the cabbie on Sixth Avenue said, someone's gotta get it; and late in the day someone does.

I am walking along Eighth Avenue during the five o'clock crush, day-dreaming, and somewhere in the forties, I don't notice the light turning red. Halfway into the path of an oncoming truck, I am lifted off my feet by a pair of hands on my upper arms and pulled back onto the curb. The hands do not release me immediately. I am pressed to the chest of the person to whom the hands belong. I can still feel the beating heart against my back. When I turn to thank my rescuer, I am looking into the middle-aged face of an overweight man with bright blue eyes, straw-colored hair, and a beet-red face. We stare wordlessly at one another. I'll never know what the man is thinking at this moment, but the expression on his face is unforgettable. Me, I am merely shaken, but he looks as though transfigured by what has just happened. His eyes are fixed on mine, but I see that they are really looking inward. I realize that this is *his* experience, not mine. It is he who has felt the urgency of life—he is still holding it in his hands.

Two hours later I am home, having dinner at my table, overlooking the city. My mind flashes on all who crossed my path today. I hear their voices, I see their gestures, I start filling in lives for them. Soon they are company, great company. I think to myself, I'd rather be here with you tonight than with anyone else I know. Well, almost anyone else I know. I look up at the great clock on my wall, the one that gives the date as well as the hour. It's time to call Leonard.

The Plimpton Prize for Fiction

is an annual award of $10,000 given to an emerging
writer whose work has appeared in *The Paris Review*.
The prize is named for the *Review*'s longtime editor,
George Plimpton, and reflects his commitment
to discovering new writers of exceptional merit.
Past recipients include Jesse Ball, Amie Barrodale,
Caitlin Horrocks, April Ayers Lawson,
Alistair Morgan, and Benjamin Percy.

Get discovered.
Submit to *The Paris Review*.

62 WHITE STREET • NEW YORK, NY 10013

CONTRIBUTORS

SYLVIE BAUMGARTEL lives in New Mexico.

PETER COLE's most recent book is *The Poetry of Kabbalah: Mystical Verse from the Jewish Tradition*. A new volume of poems, *The Invention of Influence*, is forthcoming.

ADELAIDE DOCX, an agent for classical musicians, is at work on her first novel.

STEPHEN DUNN's latest collection of poems, *Lines of Defense*, is forthcoming next year. He lives in Frostburg, Maryland.

JOHN FREEMAN is the editor of *Granta* and the author of *The Tyranny of E-mail* and *How to Read a Novelist*, forthcoming this fall.

DAVID GATES is the author of the novels *Jernigan* and *Preston Falls* and of the story collection *The Wonders of the Invisible World*.

VIVIAN GORNICK's most recent books are a biography of Emma Goldman and a collection of essays, *The Men in My Life*.

HENRY GROSSMAN, who took the original photograph of George Plimpton on our cover, has recently published the limited-edition *Places I Remember*, available from curvebender.com.

TONY HOAGLAND teaches at the University of Houston.

SAM LIPSYTE is the author of five books, most recently the story collection *The Fun Parts*.

MELCION MATEU is the author of three books of poetry: *Vida evident*, winner of the 1999 Paz Prize; *Ningú, petit*; and *Jardí amb cangurs*.

ANGE MLINKO's new collection of poems, *Marvelous Things Overheard*, is forthcoming this fall.

OTTESSA MOSHFEGH lives in Los Angeles. An early version of "Bettering Myself" appeared on the Web site twoseriousladies.org.

ROWAN RICARDO PHILLIPS is the author, most recently, of a collection of poetry, *The Ground*, and is the translator of Salvador Espriu's *Ariadne in the Grotesque Labyrinth*.

ADAM O'FALLON PRICE, his wife, and their cat live in Ithaca, New York. He is at work on his first novel.

DAVID SEARCY's first collection of essays, *Shame and Wonder*, will be published next year.

FREDERICK SEIDEL's most recent book is *Nice Weather*.

CATHERINE STEINDLER lives in Brooklyn and teaches writing at Columbia University.

TESS WHEELWRIGHT's stories have appeared in the *Yale Review*, *Crazyhorse*, and the *Massachusetts Review*.

KEVIN YOUNG is the author of seven books of poetry, including *Ardency* and *Jelly Roll: A Blues*, a finalist for the National Book Award. His most recent book is *The Grey Album: On the Blackness of Blackness*.

VVVVVVVVVVVVVVVV
EEEEEEEEEEEEEEEE
DDDDDDDDDDDDDDD
AAAAAAAAAAAAAAAA

THISISVEDA.COM

New York
Randall's Island Park
May 10 – 13, 2013

Buy Tickets Now
friezenewyork.com

'Frieze Art Fair electrifies New York'
The Wall Street Journal

'A fixture on the
international art circuit'
The New York Times

'Ground–breaking'
Financial Times

Main sponsor
Deutsche Bank

The Plimpton Circle is a remarkable group of individuals and organizations whose contributions of $1,000 or more help advance the work of The Paris Review Foundation. The Foundation gratefully acknowledges:

Donna Jo and William R. Acquavella • Keith and Peggy Anderson • Lisa Capozzi and Dave Anderson • Jeff Antebi • Winsome Brown and Claude Arpels • R. Scott Asen • Amanda Urban and Ken Auletta • René-Pierre and Alexis Azria • André Balazs • Mahnaz Ispahani Bartos and Adam Bartos • Alexandra Styron and Edward Beason • Patricia Birch Becker and William Becker • Helen and William Beekman • Robert Bell • Kate Bellin • Liz and Rod Berens • Kathryn and David Berg • Clara Bingham • Joan Bingham • The Blackstone Group • Leslie Tcheyan and Monty Blanchard • Emily Blavatnik • Ross Bleckner • Bloomberg • Lauren Schuker and Jason Blum • Suzanne Deal Booth • Livio M. Borghese • Luke Parker Bowles • Alison and George Brokaw • Stephen M. Brown • Winthrop Brown • Timothy Browne • Anne and Russell Byers • Heather Kilpatrick and Stephen Byers • Ariadne and Mario Calvo-Platero • Maria B. and Woodrow W. Campbell • Dr. Sally Peterson and Michael V. Carlisle • Lisa and Dick Cashin • Kathy Cerullo • Molly and Walter Channing • Allan Chapin • Sarah Teale and Gordon W. Chaplin • Michael Chon • City National Bank • Stephen Clark • Susanna Porter and James Clarke • Cassius Marcellus Cornelius Clay • Stacy and Eric Cochran • Daniel Cohen • Kathy Cole-Kelly • Gifford Combs • Condé Nast Traveler • Bernard F. Conners • Marianna Cook and Hans Kraus • Wendy Mackenzie and Alexander Cortesi • Georgia Cool and Christopher Cox • Hilary Cooper and Chris Crowley • Celerie Kemble and R. Boykin Curry IV • Michel David-Weill • Don DeLillo • Robert de Rothschild • Raymond Debbane • Debevoise & Plimpton LLP • Gayatri Devi • Michelle and Thomas Dewey • Leonardo DiCaprio • Diane von Furstenberg and Barry Diller • Abigail E. Disney • Jane C. Dudley • Disney Publishing Worldwide • EBSCO Publishing • Janet Ecker • Kelly and Randolph Post Eddy III • Gwen Edelman • Inger McCabe Elliott and Osborn Elliott • Rachel Cobb and Morgan Entrekin • ESPN • Harold Evans • Lise and Michael Evans • Farrar, Straus and Giroux • Jeanne Donovan Fisher • Estate of Richard B. Fisher • Wendy Stein and Bart Friedman • Arlene Hogan Fuller • Minnie Mortimer and Stephen Gaghan • Mr. and Mrs. Rowan Gaither IV • Tara Gallagher and Luke Mitchell • Martin Garbus • The David Geffen Foundation • Slavka B. Glaser • Barbara Goldsmith • Toni K. and James C. Goodale • Noah and Maria Gottdiener • Jane M. Gould • Stephen and Cathy Graham • Francine Gray • Sol Greenbaum • Michael Greenberg • The William & Mary Greve Foundation • Grove Atlantic • Grubman Indursky Shire & Meiselas, P.C. • Lawrence H. and Lucy Guffey • Mala Gaonkar • HBO • Hachette Book Group • Christina Lewis Halpern and Dan Halpern • Katharina Harf • Peter Harf • Denise and Tom Harnly • Alexander Hecker • Drue Heinz • Kathryn and John Heminway • Ken Hirsh • Franklin W. Hobbs • Christopher Hockett • Susan Levine and Wade Hooker • Sean Eldridge and Chris Hughes • Ala and Ralph Isham • Kathleen Begala and Yves-André Istel • Joele Frank, Wilkinson Brimmer Katcher • Mary Karr • Katheryn C. Patterson and Thomas L. Kempner, Jr. • Lisa Atkins and Tony Kiser • Alfred A. Knopf • Nina Köprülü • John and Duff Lambros • Fabienne and Michael Lamont • Mr. and Mrs. Stephen Langman • Sherry Lansing • Jenny Lee • Elizabeth and Jeffrey T. Leeds • Bokara Legendre • Dan Levine • Anne Kerr Kennedy and Matthew G. L'Heureux • Barbara and Robert Liberman • Gary Lippman • Hilary Mills Loomis and Robert Loomis • Renee Khatami and John R. MacArthur • Macmillan and Holtzbrinck Publishers • Chris and Kevin Madden • Alexandra and Terrence Malick • Shelby and Anthony E. Malkin • Ellen Chesler and Matt Mallow • Mr. and Mrs. Donald Marron • Peter Matthiessen • Tatiana Maxwell • Ellen and Frank McCourt • Jeanne McCulloch • Joanie McDonell • Stacey and Terry McDonell • Anne Hearst and Jay McInerney •

The Paris Review is grateful for the support of its friends. Please send your tax-deductible contribution to The Paris Review Foundation, 62 White Street, New York, NY 10013. Contact Emily Cole-Kelly at 212.343.1333 or ecolekelly@theparisreview.org.

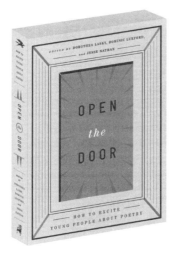
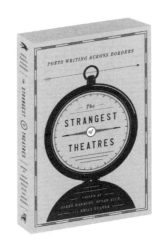

NICK VAN WOERT
NO MAN'S LAND

February 22 - April 6, 2013

OHWOW
937 N. La Cienega Blvd., Los Angeles, CA 90069
oh-wow.com

Bon Anniversaire
Paris Review

Rudolf Stingel, *Untitled (Birthday)*, 2006
oil on canvas, 15 × 20 ½ inches (38.1 × 52.1 cm)